Building
a Pacific
Community

The East-West Center is a public, non-profit educational institution with an international board of governors. Some 2,000 research fellows, graduate students, and professionals in business and government each year work with the Center's international staff in cooperative study, training, and research. They examine major issues related to population, resources and development, the environment, culture, and communication in Asia, the Pacific, and the United States. The Center was established in 1960 by the United States Congress, which provides principal funding. Support also comes from more than 20 Asian and Pacific governments, as well as private agencies and corporations.

Situated on 21 acres adjacent to the University of Hawaii's Manoa Campus, the Center's facilities include a 300-room office building housing research and administrative offices for an international staff of 250, three residence halls for participants, and a conference center with meeting rooms equipped to provide simultaneous translation and a complete range of audiovisual services.

Building a Pacific Community

The Addresses and Papers of the Pacific Community Lecture Series

Edited with an Introduction by
PAUL F. HOOPER

Foreword by
LEE-JAY CHO

Published by
The East-West Center
Distributed by
University of Hawaii Press / Honolulu

Copyright © 1982 by The East-West Center
All rights reserved.
Manufactured in the United States of America.
First printing 1982
Second printing 1987

Library of Congress Cataloging in Publication Data
Main entry under title

Building a Pacific community.

   Bibliography: p.
   1. Pan-Pacific relations—Congresses. 2. Pacific region—Economic integration—Congresses. I. Hooper, Paul F., 1938-   . II. East-West Center.
DU29.B83   337.1'9   81-17252
ISBN 0-8248-0790-1   AACR2

CONTENTS

Foreword
Lee-Jay Cho vii

Preface ix

Introduction
Paul F. Hooper 1

Addresses

Economic Cooperation in a Pacific Community
Kiyoshi Kojima 22

Building a Pacific Community
Ratu Kamisese K. T. Mara 38

ASEAN and the Pacific Region
Gerardo P. Sicat 49

Pacific Community: Dream or Reality?
John Grenfell Crawford 63

Hawaii's Role in the Pacific Community
George R. Ariyoshi 76

Prospects for a Pacific Community
Michael Mansfield 85

Papers

The Pacific Islands in a Latin American Perspective:
Towards a Special Relationship?
Francisco Orrego Vicuña 94

Changing Patterns of Trade and Trends in Trade Policy in
the Asia-Pacific Region
Nam Duck-Woo 119

Supporting Materials
    Appendix A
        Pacific Basin Regional Organizations   139
    Appendix B
        The Organization for Pacific Trade and Development Proposal   155
    Appendix C
        Summary of the Report on the Pacific Basin Cooperation Concept   167
    Selected Readings   173

FOREWORD

The East-West Center celebrated its twentieth anniversary during 1980–1981. As the Center looked forward to its third decade of service through promoting better relations and understanding among the peoples of Asia, the Pacific, and the United States, it seemed appropriate to select as its anniversary theme: "Building a Pacific Community."

This theme was selected in recognition of the significance of the idea to the nations and peoples of the East-West Center's region of interest and activity. The idea is still a new one, but it is gradually becoming an important topic of discussion and debate among the leadership and general populace of the area. Therefore, a series of lectures and papers was presented at the Center during the year to acquaint a broad range of people with various aspects of the Pacific community idea. A large number of people were reached directly during the lecture series and through reporting of the series in the local media; this book presents the speeches and papers to an even greater reading audience.

The goal of this publication is to encourage further thought and discussion of the Pacific community idea in order to promote the ideals of cooperation, understanding, and regional awareness that such a community would entail. Everyone has experienced the positive social ties and traditions of local village, town, or city communities. The idea of a community of nations in the vast Pacific region somewhat staggers the imagination, especially when one considers the great heterogeneity of cultures, languages, religions, and histories. The challenge is to explore, identify, and define some common interests around which a community can evolve.

The Center's academic work through its programs of cooperative study, training, and research in the areas of population, resources, environment, communication, and culture has clearly demonstrated that close ties already exist among various groups within the region. Professionals, scientists, scholars, businessmen, government leaders, and others already work together through specific networks of communication and organizations for cooperation. These contacts and exchanges increasingly affect the economic, social, and political well-being of the region. The Pacific community idea should promote a positive, regional sense of community and, further, should demonstrate that as the whole region is benefited, so are its parts.

I extend official and personal appreciation, as President Pro Tem of the East-West Center, both to the distinguished lecturers who expended valuable time and effort to formulate and present their views during this lecture series, and to Professor Paul F. Hooper, who edited this publication. Their contributions to the Pacific community idea mark the first steps of a long process of encouraging the collected peoples and organizations of the region to recognize their interdependent futures. It is hoped that this book will assist in the success of that endeavor.

Honolulu, Hawaii LEE-JAY CHO
April 1981

PREFACE

Longer than most people can remember, war has been the focal point of discussions on the Pacific Basin. This changed over the past decade. Now most talk concerns a burgeoning movement aimed at bringing the area together in a new regional community of nations. Incongruous as it may first appear, this surprising but heartening transposal is firmly grounded in realism. Vigorous economic growth in conjunction with relative political stability has made the Pacific Basin the center of world economic dynamism and promises to make it the focal point of virtually all global activity sometime during the coming century. With such prospects in the offing, the region's leaders are beginning to consider new arrangements better suited to cope with the emerging circumstances, and people from all quarters are quickening to the attendant excitement.

As the twentieth anniversary of the East-West Center's founding by the United States Congress in 1960 came amidst these developments, the institution chose the theme "Building a Pacific Community" for its commemoration of the occasion. Among the events staged during the year-long celebration was the Pacific Community Lecture Series, an amalgam of public lectures and scholarly papers designed to provide Pacific leaders with a forum to express their views on the regionalist movement. Lectures were delivered by George R. Ariyoshi, governor of Hawaii; John Grenfell Crawford, chancellor of the Australian National University; Kiyoshi Kojima, professor of international economics at Hitotsubashi University; Michael "Mike" Mansfield, ambassador of the United States to Japan; Ratu Kamisese K. T. Mara, prime minister of Fiji; and Gerardo P. Sicat, minister of economic planning for the Philippines. Papers were prepared by Professor Francisco Orrego Vicuña, director of the Institute of International Studies at the University of Chile; and Nam Duck-Woo, prime minister of the Republic of Korea. A third paper prepared by a Soviet scholar was unavailable at press time.

As the purpose of this book is to circulate the views of these individuals, their addresses and papers are reproduced in full in the following section. The end product is a discussion of topics ranging from economics and politics to education by representatives of the area's major market economies (Japan, Australia, and the United States), small island states (Fiji), newly industrialized countries (South Korea), regional organizations (the Association of South East Asian Nations as informally represented by the Philippines), and oft-ignored Latin American powers (Chile). Only a Marxist perspective is missing.

The Center sponsored this series because it is persuaded that the regionalist movement serves the interests of the Pacific nations and, concomitantly, that it should do what it can to assist progress within the movement. Center officials are aware that such ends will come neither quickly nor easily. They recognize that many of the factors responsible for the growth of regionalism elsewhere in the world—particularly cultural and economic homogeneity, military unity, and centralized development efforts—are essentially non-existent in the Pacific. At the same time, however, they also recognize that the nations of the Pacific, increasingly interdependent and by no means totally without experience in regional cooperation, do share certain common interests which in turn constitute a basis for developing closer relationships. They believe that a careful exploration of these points of commonality will expedite progress toward new understandings and arrangements and hope this series will contribute to that process.

Some may be surprised to find the Center, primarily an educational and research institution, collaterally involved with governments and other utilitarian organizations in promoting Pacific regional unity. In fact, such activity is entirely in character. Founded by Congress with the charge of promoting a practical exchange of ideas and techniques between East and West, the Center has consistently undertaken projects at least tangentially relevant to Pacific regionalism and on occasion has sponsored programs directly pertinent to the movement. As Professor Kojima notes at the outset of his address, his own ideas on the subject, long acknowledged for their pioneering impact, first began to take shape at a Center-sponsored conference on regional economic cooperation held in 1964.

The Center's location in Hawaii, a salient of international activism in the Pacific for well over a century, is also a factor in its involvement. Beginning with several efforts during the middle years of the nineteenth century to forge a grand confederation of Polynesian nations, Hawaiian leaders developed a commitment to internationalism that in time became one of the Islands' more distinctive characteristics. Over the years this concern resulted in such activities as the annexation of a distant island group, the first around-the-world voyage by a reigning monarch, the prospect of war with Germany, the formation of the immensely influential Institute of Pacific Relations, the emergence of the University of Hawaii as one of the nation's more important centers of international education, the creation of a league of Asian and Pacific municipal governments, and the establishment of what amounted to a local office of foreign affairs. In short, an international consciousness evolved in Hawaii that has made response to developments elsewhere in the Pacific almost instinctive. Like so many other Island institutions, the Center, too, has been profoundly influenced by this milieu.

Many contributed to the Pacific Community Lecture Series and to this book. Their efforts cannot go unacknowledged. The greatest debt is owed those who took time from onerous schedules to speak in the series and prepare papers for it. In large measure they are responsible for its success as a stimulant to thought and, one hopes, action.

Credit for the success of the undertaking is also due numerous Center officials who contributed immense amounts of time and energy with unfailing good spirit. President Pro Tem Lee-Jay Cho, his predecessor Everett Kleinjans, Board of Governors member George Kanahele, Dean of Student Affairs and Open Grants Sumi Makey, Assistant to the President Richard R. Vuylsteke, and especially Corporation Secretary Robert B. Hewett devoted countless hours to the program. Staff members Jeannette Bennington, eLena Javinar, Grace S. Kohatsu, and Susan Okano, among others, did likewise.

Support for the series also came from outside the Center. In the first instance, the hundreds of individuals who attended the lectures made the entire effort seem worthwhile. Still others—several of whom require special mention—were more than generous with their particular talents. George Chaplin, editor-in-chief of the *Honolulu Advertiser*, assisted the program with good advice and informed reporting. Sandi Carney of television station KITV was equally helpful with her reporting. The late Wilson P. Cannon of the Bank of Hawaii was a major source of ideas and encouragement before his untimely passing. Everyone associated with the series misses him.

This book is likewise the product of much good assistance and advice. Chancellor Crawford and Professor Kojima ever so kindly consented to read the manuscript of the introduction, and both responded with excellent suggestions. Fusae Uyemura and Miriam Gould of the Center staff were unfailingly available to type interminable drafts of the manuscript. Finally, Alison Mito compiled statistics, checked data, typed manuscript, and read proof with keen insight and constant good cheer.

These people have my lasting gratitude. While I accept responsibility for the book's faults, they deserve much of the credit for its strengths.

P. F. H.

Building
a Pacific
Community

INTRODUCTION

At some point during the past decade the center of global economic dynamism shifted from the North Atlantic to the Pacific Basin. Dramatic as this transition was—it is at least as significant as the earlier shift of the economic center from the Mediterranean to Northern Europe and, subsequently, the North Atlantic—few people in a world accustomed to thinking in Atlantic terms were more than dimly aware of it, and fewer still realized that it involved anything more basic than trade disputes between Japan and the West.[1] More regrettable, after almost a decade of increasingly focused discussion of the subject, there is little to suggest that people outside the Pacific Basin are much more aware of the new circumstances than they were at the outset.

Such provincialism is unfortunate as it obscures a host of modern global economic realities. Most significant in this regard is the fact that the collective economic strength of the Pacific Basin now exceeds that of the North Atlantic region. Even if the region's socialist economies, Pacific slope Latin American powers, and Pacific Island nations are excluded from the equation, there is still a rough equivalency between the two areas. Put otherwise, the collective economic strength of Japan, South Korea, Taiwan, Hong Kong, the Philippines, Thailand, Malaysia, Singapore, Indonesia, Australia, and New Zealand plus Canada and the United States now approximates that of Western Europe plus Canada and the United States. Add the remaining nations of the Pacific Basin and the region is unquestionably the new center of world economic activity.

This circumstance is due largely to the fact that the nations of the Pacific region now equal or exceed those of the Atlantic in such basic matters as population growth, food production, mineral resource extraction, economic development, and foreign trade expansion. Representative data illustrate these developments. As regards population, the area's total has long exceeded that of any other region on earth. With Australia, New Zealand, Canada, and the United States among the world's leading agricultural powers, the same is true with respect to food production. Similarly, the region's share in the extraction of important minerals is high. For example, it produces some 80 percent of the world's nickel, 65 percent of its iron ore, 60 percent of its uranium and tin, 54 percent of its zinc and bauxites, 49 percent of its copper, 47 percent of its silver, and 46 percent of its coal. Combined, these factors constitute the essence of the region's current dynamism and future potential.

Leaving aside the Organization of Petroleum Exporting Countries (OPEC) nations, the developing countries of the Pacific have led the world in economic growth rates for the better part of the past two decades. During the 1965–1973 period, for example, Singapore ranked first, South Korea third, and Taiwan fifth, all at annual rates exceeding 10 percent. Perhaps even more noteworthy, during the same era Japan, a fully developed and industrialized nation, grew at something over 4 percent per annum, or approximately twice the rate of the most vital industrial powers elsewhere in the world. As a consequence roughly a third of all world trade now occurs within the Pacific, and it is growing at an annual rate that surpasses rates in other parts of the world by nearly 10 percent. In dollar terms the volume of this exchange swelled from around US$40 billion in 1960 to US$380 billion in 1978.

Such changes are in large part the result of Japan's recent emergence as a major economic force and the concomitant rise of her principal Asian trading partners to positions of consequence. In 1969, little more than two decades after the devastation of World War II, Japan became the world's third-ranking economic power, trailing only the United States and the Soviet Union, and current statistics indicate that a second place ranking is imminent. Buoyed by this vitality, Japan's East and Southeast Asian economic allies have enjoyed recent growth rates ranging from still healthy lows of around 5 percent per annum to unparalleled highs of over 10 percent. The particular nature of this growth has wrought a fundamental change in the nature of regional economic relations. Based to an extraordinary degree upon region-wide, intra-industrial trade as opposed to more traditional bilateral import-export activity, Japanese and Japanese-inspired growth has transformed the western Pacific and, to a lesser extent, the entire Pacific into an interdependent economic web where regional cooperation is rapidly becoming necessary as a matter of survival.[2] So it is that many have come to view the formation of a regional entity as not only desirable but imperative.

The degree to which these nations have in fact become bound together in such a web—the extent to which decisions that were once largely of domestic consequence now affect the entire region—became evident in the course of several unfortunate conflicts that occurred during the 1970s. The continuing failure of Japan and the United States to consult one another properly on problems relative to such high-trade items as soybeans, textiles, automobiles, and steel has produced the current spectre of a protectionist war capable of shattering the economic vitality of the entire region. Unilateral decisions by Thailand during 1973-1974 with respect to embargoing rice exports, by South Korea in 1974 regarding the devaluation of the *won*, and by Australia during 1975-1976 concerning restrictions upon certain Asian imports disrupted supply, financial, and trade arrangements across a wide area. Equally singular decisions by the United States in 1972 with respect to the normalization of relations with the People's Republic of China and in 1976 regarding the withdrawal of troops from South Korea provoked similar repercussions on the political front.[3] In other words, these nations, all key contributors to the economic dynamism of the region, have on occasion acted as if they were more independent than interdependent, and there were no institutional arrangements in force capable of persuading them to act otherwise. The various United Nations agencies and independent subregional organizations proved to be either too general or too limited. More than a few are beginning to wonder how much longer the margins for error can continue to absorb such mistakes.

A proper explication of the region's dynamism involves still other elements. One of the most important is the fact that the United States redefined its strategic interests in the area over the past decade, in the process replacing an earlier and rather narrow concern for military security with a more complex set of considerations based to a much greater degree upon economic relations. This change is evident in recent trade and investment statistics. In contrast with figures from a decade ago, some 40 percent of America's trade now takes place in the Pacific. Essentially a two-way traffic in raw materials, foodstuffs, and high-technology industrial products, the volume of this exchange has surpassed that of trade across the Atlantic and is still growing. Further, direct investment in the Pacific by American corporations, once dominant but then surpassed by that of Japanese firms, is again on the increase and approaching competitive levels. At present, it totals some US$16 billion and accounts for approximately 30 percent of all foreign investment in the region. Comparable figures for Japanese corporations are US$21.5 billion and 40 percent.

As a consequence of these and still other related developments the region's major market powers have experienced an unprecedented convergence of interests with respect to maintaining a rational and open economic order. Unsurprisingly, they are also discovering a concern for new regional institutions capable of protecting and expanding that order.[4] So it is that the Pacific has become the center of contemporary economic dynamism and the crucible for the world's newest experiment with regionalism.

While all too few paid the Pacific economic drama of the past several decades much heed, there were those who grasped what was afoot and understood that the new circumstances would, sooner or later, necessitate new arrangements within the region. Worried as well as excited by these changes, a small and essentially unorganized but nonetheless influential group of scholars, political leaders, and entrepreneurs from around the Pacific initiated an informal dialogue. With time, they came to the general conclusion that some form of common regional action embracing new visions, practices, and, in all probability, institutions would be necessary to assure any degree of long-term stability. Although aware that such factors as cultural heterogeneity, historical dissimilitude, national rivalry, economic disparity, and physical separation rendered their objectives difficult in the extreme, they began to address the concept of regionalism and propose a variety of undertakings calculated to foster its growth.

Examples of this loosely knit group's endeavors abound. In

Introduction

the scholarly realm, the source of most initial activity, Professor Kiyoshi Kojima and Hiroshi Kurimoto published an article in 1966 which called upon the nations of the Pacific to join together in a free-trade area similar to the European Economic Community.[5] Although subsequently criticized for suggesting restrictive economic arrangements and rendered largely irrelevant by the continued success of the General Agreement on Tariffs and Trade in reducing trade barriers throughout the area, their proposal is often cited as the genesis of current interest in Pacific Basin regionalism.

This study was but the first of many to come from scholarly sources. Academicians from the region, particularly those from Japan, Australia, and the United States, took up the subject and wrote on it at length. Their interest led to the formation of several scholarly journals, the most significant being *Asia Pacific Community* (originally *Pacific Community*) which was founded in Tokyo in 1969 and is the source of numerous subsequent articles concerning the concept of community in the Pacific.[6] Monographs and books also began to appear. For the most part highly technical and directed at specialized audiences, some gained a broad readership. A case in point is futurist Herman Kahn's 1971 study entitled *The Emerging Japanese Superstate*, which, among other things, offered the then startling prediction that the Pacific was destined to assume the pivotal role in world affairs once held by the Mediterranean and, later, the North Atlantic.[7]

Scholarly interest in Pacific regionalism soon found its way into the political arena. In one of the earliest instances, Japanese Foreign Minister (and later Prime Minister) Takeo Miki, attracted by an earlier version of the Kojima-Kurimoto study, lent support to an informal gathering of academic and government economists which was convened early in 1968 to explore regional trade and development issues. Inspired by the exchange of views, the participants themselves organized a subsequent gathering which in turn led to a continuing series of meetings now known as the Pacific Trade and Development Conferences (PAFTAD). Largely academic in nature, these meetings have since produced an important body of scholarship on a number of regional issues and are responsible for developing a cadre of scholarly authorities now in the fore of virtually every major aspect of the Pacific regionalist movement.[8]

Foreign Minister Miki was not the only political figure attracted to the movement during the early years. Although less active, a number of his contemporaries—among them United States President Richard M. Nixon and Japanese Prime Minister Eisaku Sato—are also on record in support of at least the general concept.[9] Still further support came from those who took the lead in forming such new regional and subregional organizations as the Asian Development Bank in 1965, the Association of South East Asian Nations (ASEAN) in 1967, and the South Pacific Bureau for Economic Cooperation in 1973.[10] (See Appendix A for a more complete listing of regional organizations.) While these organizations were designed to serve specific purposes, they nonetheless contributed to the growing sense of community within the region and inspired thoughts of still more ambitious institutional undertakings. ASEAN, for example, is now frequently cited as an appropriate model for a Pacific-wide organizational effort.

Pacific Basin business leaders likewise became interested in the regionalist movement during the 1960s. In 1967 officers of a number of important financial, trading, and manufacturing concerns from the industrialized nations of the area formed the Pacific Basin Economic Council to facilitate consultation on regional economic matters. Meeting regularly over the years, the group has expanded to some four hundred firms representing most of the nations of the area and is among the major supporters of the current regionalist movement.[11] A year later, American Chambers of Commerce within the region joined together in the Asia-Pacific Council of American Chambers of Commerce in an effort to similarly stimulate broad consultation.[12] Hence, private entrepreneurial activism took its place alongside that emerging from the academic and political sectors.

Despite the general lack of notice from a public more concerned with such matters as the war in Vietnam and trade competition between Japan and the United States, efforts to forge a new Pacific regional consciousness continued apace into the 1970s. The major activities of the preceding years continued, and a variety of new undertakings arose. Although largely independent of the initial circles of endeavor, the newer ventures nonetheless fall into the same general academic, governmental, and independent categories of activity. Again, representative examples abound.

With respect to scholarship, the Australian National Univer-

Introduction 7

sity has emerged as a major center of Pacific regionalist study largely as a result of the work of Chancellor John Grenfell Crawford and Peter Drysdale, activist scholars now widely recognized as leading authorities on the subject. In addition, the school has sponsored a number of important conferences over the last several years, the most recent being a major gathering during September 1980 which involved key governmental and academic figures from throughout the region and produced intense debate over proposals to create a formal, government-backed regional entity. Chancellor Crawford's address reports in detail on the proceedings.[13] In similar fashion, a seminar on Canadian-American business relations hosted by the University of Washington in 1974 grew into a continuing research and instruction program focused upon Pacific Basin economic and political issues. Entitled the Pacific Rim Project, this program has since sponsored an impressive number of technical studies, cross-cultural training seminars for area business leaders, and lectures by prominent figures in the regionalist movement.[14]

The think tanks likewise became involved with the movement during these years. The Japan Economic Research Center, to cite an important case in point, has long supported PAFTAD activities through publication of its conference proceedings and sponsorship of its research. Similarly, the Brookings Institution has supported the work of interested scholars from the United States, particularly that of Lawrence B. Krause, who is among the most prominent of the American authorities on Pacific regionalism. More recently, the Aspen Institute for Humanistic Studies initiated a series of policy workshops dealing with Pacific marine resources, energy and industrial development, communications, and institutional development, and the prestigious Nomura Research Institute likewise took up the cause when it endorsed the concept of a Pacific regional organization.[15]

Within the political sphere, the government of Hawaii, long an enthusiastic advocate of internationalism, has been the principal backer of regionalist activity during most of this period. With few exceptions, its leaders have consistently supported the concept through both rhetoric and action. In 1970, the state sponsored a much-publicized futures planning conference which issued a final report urging, among other things, that the nations of the Pacific join together in a vast consultative network built around a series of new regional institutions concerned with education, communications, tourism, the arts, and commerce. More to the point, the report proposed the prompt formation of an international committee to undertake the requisite organizational tasks.[16]

While the committee itself never materialized, the proposal excited enough local interest to sustain a lively community dialogue which, in time, did lead to action. In 1974 George Kanahele and Michael Haas, international activists who participated in the conference and the subsequent discussions, published an article in *Pacific Community* which argued that the time for new undertakings had arrived and that a series of organizational activities similar to those proposed by the conference should be initiated forthwith.[17] Shortly thereafter they formed committees in Hawaii and Japan as the vanguard of a region-wide effort.[18] Although the Hawaiian group functioned only briefly, the Japanese group, formally entitled the Pacific Council of Japan and led by Ato Masuda of Waseda University, has remained active. It is presently assisting with the formation of a similar group in Indonesia.[19] More recent activities resulting at least in part from Hawaii's enthusiasm for this cause include some of the Pacific's most extensive media reportage of the regionalist movement, a pledge from Governor Ariyoshi—delivered as part of his address in this lecture series—to provide institutional support for the movement, and the lecture series itself.[20]

The independent realm has also been the scene of lively activity. Although less prominently noticed than similar earlier endeavors, a variety of new and essentially private regional institutions have been organized in recent years. Among the more noteworthy is the Pacific Forum, an independent international organization formed in Hawaii to bring academicians, government officials, and business leaders together for periodic seminars on current policy issues in the Pacific.[21] Like so many other organizations, this group has come to advocate the creation of a new regional entity and hopes to play a significant role in its planning. In the wake of extensive hearings on Pacific regionalism held during 1979, United States Congressman Lester Wolff, chairman of the Subcommittee on Pacific Affairs of the House of Representatives Committee on Foreign Affairs, established a similar group called the Pan-Pacific Community Association.[22] It continues to be active despite Congressman Wolff's defeat in the 1980 elections. In

Introduction   9

1979 a number of university, government, and corporate telecommunications professionals from throughout the Pacific (including, contrary to the usual rule, Latin America) met to explore common problems and, much like the participants in the original PAFTAD gathering a decade earlier, concluded that subsequent gatherings would be useful. Accordingly, in 1980 they formed the Pacific Telecommunications Council, a unique blend of institutions and individuals from both the public and private sectors which may well provide a useful structural model for other ventures still to come.[23]

Significant as these and related endeavors may prove to be, several recent and much-publicized initiatives on the part of governmental leaders in the United States and Japan are attracting nearly all current attention. They involve a United States Senate subcommittee report urging the nations of the Pacific to join together in a regional trade and development organization and an unofficial report prepared for the prime minister of Japan recommending a somewhat similar course of action. As these papers suggest that the two most important governments of the Pacific, hitherto only peripherally concerned with regionalism, may now be preparing to formally endorse the movement, they have generated considerable excitement.

To elaborate, in mid-1979, Hugh Patrick of Yale University and Peter Drysdale of the Australian National University, working at the request of Senator John Glenn, then chairman of the Subcommittee on East Asian and Pacific Affairs of the Senate Committee on Foreign Relations, completed a proposal calling for the formation of a new Pacific regional entity to be known as the Organization for Pacific Trade and Development (OPTAD). Based upon ideas developed in the course of earlier PAFTAD meetings, this proposal envisions a loose association of the region's five major developed market economies (Japan, Australia, New Zealand, Canada, and the United States) and nine developing market economies (South Korea, Taiwan, Hong Kong, the five members of ASEAN, and Papua New Guinea) in concert with certain small Pacific Island nations for purposes of institutionalized consultation on trade, developmental aid, and long-term economic planning. It recommends that participation by the remaining nations of the region—the socialist states as well as those of South Asia and Latin America—be delayed at least until the formative steps are completed. More specifically, the proposal recommends the creation of a steering committee composed of all participants, a secretariat, and six permanent task forces concerned with free trade, trade procedure restructuring, developmental aid, direct foreign investment, resource and energy security, and relations with the socialist states. (See Appendix B for the essential portion of the proposal.) In general terms, the proposed organization is in effect a regional version of the big power-oriented Organization for Economic Cooperation and Development which was formed in 1960 by the various Marshall Plan participants and subsequently expanded to include Japan (1964), Finland (1969), Australia (1971), and New Zealand (1973).

Shortly after the Patrick-Drysdale proposal was released, a similar if somewhat more vague proposal was issued in Japan. Its roots date generally to a long-time concern for internationalism that gradually evolved into a major theme in Japanese domestic politics and specifically to remarks about the desirability of regional cooperation made by the late Masayoshi Ohira during his campaign for the prime ministership in 1978. Upon taking office, the new prime minister established an informal, ad hoc committee called the Pacific Basin Cooperation Study Group to explore the question of Pacific regionalism and recommend ways of strengthening mutual understanding and economic cooperation throughout the area. Initially led by Saburo Okita, the distinguished economist and well-known advocate of regionalism (who subsequently resigned the position to become foreign minister in the Ohira government), the group produced an interim report late in 1979 and full report in mid-1980. Despite certain generalities, it is apparent that the authors of this report envision ends similar to those suggested in the Patrick-Drysdale proposal. However, their major emphasis is placed upon a complex of educational and research programs designed to augment the activities of a trade and development organization and, more broadly, to foster a sense of internationalism within Japan and throughout the region. (See Appendix C for a summary of the proposal.)

In addition to raising hopes within the movement, these documents have also raised a number of potentially troublesome questions, several of which require comment. In the first instance, while both papers hint at formal governmental support for the current regionalist movement, neither in fact carries any degree of

Introduction 11

official endorsement. Both have thus tended to generate overly optimistic expectations. Further, in forcefully arguing that participation in a new regional entity would serve the national interests of the United States, the Patrick-Drysdale report has aroused considerable suspicion throughout Asia with respect to American intent.[24] Conversely, Japan's rather consistent reluctance to take bold international initiatives in the years since World War II has led many to wonder about her willingness to vigorously support such objectives should they someday become institutionalized.[25] These concerns, however, have detracted little from the growing sense that the two major powers of the area are moving toward a closer identification with the regionalist movement and that the coming decade cannot help but be one of accelerated and fruitful activity.

Such enthusiasm reached unprecedented heights during mid-1980. Buoyed by an onslaught of friendly media reports, a host of supportive editorial opinions, and a growing volume of public discussion, some advocates were moved to speculate that a new regional body, and simultaneously a new age in the Pacific, would in fact be structured within the near future. Then events conspired to dampen the exuberance. First, Prime Minister Ohira's passing slowed the pace of developments in Japan despite the fact that his successor, Zenko Suzuki, was quick to express personal approval of the movement and undertake a round of related diplomatic activities. Similarly, the success of the Republicans in the 1980 elections raised as yet unanswered questions about continued support for the concept within the United States. Even more to the point, the September meeting at the Australian National University—a gathering some had hoped would prepare the way for prompt organizational decisions as it was supported by both the Australian and Japanese governments—evolved into a forum for the expression of small power concerns about the likely loss of identity should they join a regional organization dominated by big powers. While there was no rejection of the concept of regionalism, many questions were raised with respect to the existing proposals, and it became clear that there was little sentiment favoring any hurried conclusions. As a consequence, the only "organizational decision" to emerge from the meeting was a recommendation that supporters of the concept, acting in a private and unofficial capacity, form a standing Pacific Cooperation Committee and, in turn, establish separate task forces to investigate problems relative to trade, direct investment, energy, marine resources, and such international services as transportation, communication, and educational exchange. It was also suggested that the committee take responsibility for arranging subsequent gatherings.[26]

Although disappointing to many, this turn of events may eventually prove advantageous. As is now evident to all, there are numerous troublesome questions which must be resolved before any new order can arise in the Pacific, and the cautious, process-oriented approach recommended by the Canberra gathering appears well suited to these circumstances. Success, however, is in no wise guaranteed, as the questions which must first be answered—for the most part related to matters of institutional function and form—are profound and complex. Indeed, even the selection of a starting point is fraught with major consequences. Should initial efforts be devoted to a resolution of functional questions, the options with respect to form will be limited. Conversely, a decision to concentrate first upon matters of form will circumscribe the functional options.

For better or worse, it is increasingly apparent that the starting point issue has in large measure already been resolved. As indicated by the focus of all the major proposals and position papers, the vast majority of the literature, and most of the public commentary (including all the addresses in this series with the rather noteworthy exception of the two delivered by Pacific Island leaders), there is an emerging consensus that the movement must be anchored upon functional issues and that the most important single issue in this respect is economic cooperation. Therefore, barring a radical alteration of positions, the likely thrust of any further organizational activity is evident.

Should this decision be formalized, a host of potential organizational foci, which at least some feel deserve further consideration, almost certainly will be bypassed. They include military security, political unification, cultural and academic cooperation, and regional communications development. While it may well be, as proponents of the economic focus argue, that such objectives are either politically unachievable or functionally unessential, the fact remains that none of them is likely to receive more than cursory attention despite the conviction of certain key figures that the

Introduction 13

emerging economic consensus is ill-advised. Governor Ariyoshi's emphasis upon the importance of educational cooperation in his address is a case in point.

Even if a general consensus regarding economic cooperation should materialize, a number of perplexing problems will remain. In the first instance, the planners will have to resolve questions relative to the particular kind of economic activity desired. As noted, earlier debate centered around the desirability of establishing a regional trading organization akin to the European Economic Community. While this possibility has since been rejected by virtually all concerned as incompatible with the commitment of Japan and the United States to open trade and unnecessary in the face of gains realized under the General Agreement on Tariffs and Trade, an equally baffling question has arisen in its place. Should primary emphasis in any new undertaking be placed upon the promotion of trade and investment or upon the provision of grants and loans—foreign aid—for developmental assistance programs? The Patrick-Drysdale proposal addresses both options but with a clear preference for the former. In large part, this reflects the reemerging view that a thriving economic climate may, after all, be the most effective means of nurturing development. Prime Minister Nam's paper supports this argument with considerable passion.

In accord with recent foreign policy shifts, the Japanese report places considerably greater emphasis upon issues pertinent to developmental assistance. This is particularly evident in its discussion of educational and research programs. Professor Kojima's rather detailed proposal in his address for a revolving aid fund designed to increase the effectiveness of current aid programs by revising existing bilateral arrangements further illustrates this concern. Hence, the Japanese position, while generally similar to that of the Patrick-Drysdale proposal, is likely to force considerable debate over the proper balance between trade and investment programs and developmental assistance programs before any final organizational decision can be made.

Should the planners decide to emphasize developmental assistance, still further decisions will be required with respect to the actual nature of that aid. Although less the case in Asia and the Pacific than in other areas of the developing world, inadequate food production, growing social tensions, rising urban employment, limited energy resources, raging inflation, pyramiding environmental problems, and crushing debt loads in conjunction with burgeoning population growth rates have created a circumstance wherein the asymmetry between the developing and developed worlds is all too frequently on the increase. The rich are becoming richer while the poor grow poorer. Within this context, the planners will have to decide whether the traditional approach to foreign aid—a combination of public and private funds invested in the modernization of selected industries and institutions with the hope the benefits will trickle down to all segments of society—is more appropriate than the recent call by advocates of the "New International Economic Order" for a massive, direct, and long-term transfer of goods, services, and resources from the developed to the developing world, or, as current terminology has it, from the North to the South. Although viewed with extreme skepticism in many industrial nations, the latter approach must at least be pondered by any new regional organization in the Pacific. As recent studies such as the Brandt Commission's report for the World Bank and the Mitsubishi Research Institute's private report indicate, increasing numbers of serious observers are now persuaded that only direct assistance of unprecedented scope offers any promise of forestalling chaos in the developing world.[27]

This decision, essentially a matter of wrestling with the yet unresolved "how does development work" conundrum, will be difficult largely because there is little persuasive evidence that either approach is capable of resolving the dilemma. Time has shown that the traditional approach can bring substantial changes to a developing nation but usually at the price of creating sharp societal divisions. As high technology–low labor techniques replace the older low technology–high labor procedures, new classes of urban elites and urban poor are created. While subsequent sociopolitical reforms may resolve this dilemma, as happened in most of the original industrial nations, many question whether there is sufficient time for the same process to work itself through again in the developing world. The assorted pressures noted earlier may be too intense. At the same time, the more ambitious and as yet untried approach is encountering extreme resistance from an industrial world plagued by inflation, declining productivity, and growing skepticism about the efficacy of all developmental programs. It is not uncommon to find serious commentators remarking that the entire new economic order issue is little more than a Third World attempt to shift the blame for its own failings to the industrial world and should, therefore, be paid little serious attention.[28]

To the extent that developmental assistance statistics are an indication, such a view is already in the ascendant even with respect to existing aid programs. The percentage of gross national product contributed to such programs by the principal industrialized market powers is presently about half what it was two decades ago, and other nations have yet to fill the void. The Soviet Union, always cautious with its aid, has not done so, and the oil producing bloc, a group obviously capable of greater support, has actually reduced the total amount of its assistance over the past several years.[29] An alternate approach would doubtlessly be welcome, but suggestions to date, largely centered around concepts of limited growth and appropriate technology, have sparked no widespread enthusiasm in either the North or the South.

Under these circumstances, it is understandable that some, including those who drafted the Patrick-Drysdale proposal, have chosen to de-emphasize the entire issue of developmental assistance and instead place their faith in the seemingly timeless strategy of development through trade and investment. However, even this approach, simple and proven as it is, carries no guarantees of workability within the Pacific Basin given its complex blend of economic unity with physical, social, economic, and political diversity. Clearly, then, reductive as a decision to focus the regional movement upon economic cooperation may be, it will still leave a host of difficult ancillary questions unanswered.

A decision to proceed along a particular functional line will of course limit the structural as well as functional options available to the movement. This means that some interesting structural proposals will have to be shunted aside. A recent suggestion that the many existing regional organizations in the Pacific be melded together in a loose deliberative body is a case in point. Such an undertaking would provide the physically and culturally diverse region with a ready-made forum—complete with an existing membership, financial base, and communications network—for more extensive consultation and planning than has occurred to date.[30] It would also answer those critics who hold, perhaps rightly, that the movement's present leadership is too narrowly drawn. While it would create an organization so disparate in perspective and interest that even the adoption of a discussion agenda might prove difficult, it would certainly foster the kind of creative ambiguity some feel is an essential prerequisite to any successful organizational effort.[31]

In a more focused version of the same suggestion, others have argued that the various *economic* organizations presently active in the region should be encouraged to coordinate their endeavors as the initial step toward structural unity. The particular advantage of this approach, advocates say, is that it avoids still another layer of bureaucracy.[32] Among the organizations mentioned in this respect are the Organization for Economic Cooperation and Development (as it now has a Pacific membership), such United Nations agencies as the Economic and Social Commission for Asia and the Pacific and the United Nations Conference on Trade and Development, and such regional groups as the Asian Development Bank, the Pacific Basin Economic Council, and ASEAN. Engaging as this thought may be, it has yet to inspire much excitement among movement activists.[33] They perceive the global institutions as too broadly composed and too casually associated with the Pacific to serve the more specific ends of a distinctly regional organization. In the same breath, they characterize the existing regional groups as too narrowly composed and focused, a point that at least one of those groups—the Pacific Basin Economic Council—is quick to acknowledge.[34]

This dismissal appears hasty in at least the case of ASEAN, as its purpose and structure are clearly akin to those envisaged by most movement planners. Indeed, the Patrick-Drysdale proposal stresses the importance of a special relationship with this group, and some have suggested that it serve as both the model and the precipitant for the movement. However, there are many who feel this would be inadvisable. They find the group too subregional in perspective and too involved with local issues to assume an expanded role.[35] As Minister Sicat notes in his address, there is a tendency within the organization itself to agree with this assessment, as there is fear that any closer association with the other powers of the region would necessarily result in a submergence of its own more immediate economic and political interests. As in prior instances, then, limited as the movement's structural options may be, they are still sufficient to confound and no doubt protract the planning process.

Introduction   17

Questions of form and function also have a bearing upon the matter of leadership and participation, an issue that has already generated some controversy and will surely be responsible for more in the future. Here, too, prior decisions effectively limit the options. If, for example, there is a firm decision to proceed along economic lines—particularly if it is decided to follow the basic recommendations of the Patrick-Drysdale proposal—there can be little doubt that Japan and the United States will provide most of the leadership and that initial participation will be restricted to the North American, East Asian, and Southeast Asian market economies. South Asian, Latin American, and socialist bloc participation could follow, but there is no assurance that it would. As much as different arrangements might be desirable in the interest of the broadest possible participation, it is unlikely they could be made without an extensive reformulation of the basic proposal.

This conclusion is of course predicated upon the assumption that the existing proposals and position papers accurately project future developments. As the Canberra gathering and Chancellor Crawford's address make clear, such an assumption is now tenuous. These proposals and papers are at best informal and preliminary, and, as Ambassador Mansfield notes in his address, both Japan and the United States are increasingly reluctant to press them for fear of further alienating the already skeptical smaller nations of the region. Further, with what movement advocates must surely consider more than a touch of paranoia, certain figures from the smaller nations are now suggesting that the very need for a new regional entity be reconsidered, and some are beginning to wonder if such an undertaking might be little more than a screen for Japanese and American hopes of establishing greater control over the area. A few have even gone so far as to conjecture about a linkage between regionalism and neo-colonialism. On more than one occasion reference to Japan's World War II era Greater East Asia Co-Prosperity Sphere has slipped into the conversation.[36] As Prime Minister Ratu Mara's address indicates, this concern extends well beyond any radical fringe to include some of the region's most respected leaders.

There are still other dimensions to the leadership and participation issue. In contrast with the worries of the smaller nations about forced participation, others are beginning to wonder about their apparent exclusion from participation. As Professor Orrego's paper suggests, this is true of the Pacific slope nations of Latin

America. More ominously, it is also true of the major socialist powers. Without doubt, the Soviet Union considers itself a Pacific power and expects to have some say with respect to any significant new developments in the region, a fact that promises to inject certain geopolitical considerations into the discussions. Such considerations will become an even greater issue when—and the time will surely arrive—participation by the People's Republic of China is proposed. For a variety of well-known reasons, neither Japan nor the United States is likely to risk alienating China. Hence, should that nation seek a role in any new organization, it would almost certainly be forthcoming despite the problems such a step would present with respect to relations with Taiwan and the Soviet Union. While there has as yet been no formal expression of interest from Beijing, Prime Minister Ohira addressed the possibility of Chinese participation on several occasions prior to his death, and it can safely be assumed that the matter will arise again. In still another instance, then, a series of extremely troublesome issues will have to be resolved before theory can become action.

There can be little doubt that the future of Pacific regionalism is presently shrouded in uncertainty. If anything is apparent at this point, it is that a multitude of extraordinarily complex issues —each with ramifications far beyond those readily apparent— must be debated and properly resolved before any viable new organizational arrangements are likely to emerge. Despite noteworthy recent progress, there is as yet no cause for euphoria.

Still, advocates of Pacific regionalism can applaud events of late. Two decades previous the very concept of a regional movement was unfamiliar to all but a handful of individuals. Now it is a matter of considerable interest to thousands, including many who hold key positions in academia, government, the media, and business. As recently as the last decade, even the most ardent supporters of the concept were only dimly aware of the range and nature of the pertinent issues. Now these issues are largely defined and an impressive array of scholars, public officials, and private planners is engaged in the task of finding appropriate solutions. Finally, only several years ago there was nothing even approximating a mechanism for bringing concerned individuals and groups together in consultation and research. Now there are many, and still another is forming—the Pacific Cooperative

Committee—which may someday bring the work of all the others together in a grand synthesis. The agenda for action suggested for this group at Canberra, coupled with Governor Ariyoshi's subsequent offer of financial support, makes this prospect all the more likely. Clearly, the future is hopeful.

In addition to such tangible developments, there is also a sense that time is on the side of the movement. The Pacific—dynamic, changing, and optimistic—may at last be poised to fulfill American Secretary of State William Henry Seward's mid-nineteenth-century prophecy that it would become the "chief theatre of events in the world's great hereafter," and the regionalist movement may well be the vehicle that will bring this dream to pass. As the regionalist urge in the Pacific and elsewhere illustrates, the era of the nation-state seems to be running its course, in the process making way for a new era of supranational organizations. Should such an era materialize, there are indications that it will be one characterized by institutions at least generally akin to those associated with the current regionalist movement. Internationalist thought is presently turning away from earlier notions of a vertically organized world-state as the next logical step in the progression that began with the city-state, and is looking instead toward horizontally organized regional compacts as the most effective way of dealing with a world that is at once interconnected and pluralistic. Why, as one scholar recently put it, should it be assumed that a replication of the very hierarchical, overarching institutions that have so long failed to resolve problems at the national level will somehow prove capable of resolving them at the international level?[37]

All of this is the stuff of at least guarded optimism, and supporters of the Pacific community movement have considerable justification for responding accordingly. For once, time and the course of events appear to be friends rather than foes.

NOTES

1. For further historical details, see William H. Overholt, "The Rise of the Pacific Basin," *Pacific Community*, 6, no. 4 (July 1974): 516-533.
2. Such figures are commonly cited in the literature on Pacific regionalism. For example, see U.S., Congress, Senate, Committee on Foreign Relations, *An Asian-Pacific Regional Economic Organization: An Exploratory Con-*

cept Paper, 96th Cong., 1st Sess., 1979; Endel-Jakob Kolde, *The Pacific Quest: The Concept and Scope of an Oceanic Community*, Pacific Rim Research Series, no. 1 (Lexington, Mass., 1976); and *Honolulu Advertiser*, August 10-14, 1980.

3. For greater detail, see Lawrence B. Krause, "The Pacific Economy in an Interdependent World," unpublished paper prepared at the Brookings Institution, October 1978, pp. 10-14.
4. U.S., Congress, Senate, Committee on Foreign Relations, pp. 10-12.
5. Kiyoshi Kojima and Hiroshi Kurimoto, "A Pacific Economic Community and Asian Developing Countries," *Hitotsubashi Journal of Economics*, 7 (June 1966): 17-37. Also see Kiyoshi Kojima, *Japan and a Pacific Free Trade Area* (London, 1971).
6. For representative examples, see articles by U. Alexis Johnson, Harlan Cleveland, Kiyoshi Kojima, James E. Auer, Dick Wilson, William H. Overholt, and George S. Kanahele and Michael Haas published between 1969 and 1976. There are, of course, other periodicals that occasionally publish on the Pacific community movement.
7. Herman Kahn, *The Emerging Japanese Superstate: Challenge and Response* (Englewood Cliffs, N.J., 1971).
8. For example, see Takeo Miki, *An Asian-Pacific Sphere* (Tokyo, 1967). The most pointed example is the fact that the outlines of the Patrick-Drysdale proposal were developed in these gatherings.
9. See Richard M. Nixon, "Asia After Vietnam," *Foreign Affairs*, 46, no. 1 (October 1967): 111-125; and Eisaku Sato, "Pacific Asia," *Pacific Community*, 1, no. 1 (October 1969):1-3.
10. Of course, other international and regional organizations keyed to Pacific issues existed prior to the rise of the current movement. See Appendix A for a reasonably complete listing.
11. U.S., Congress, Senate, Committee on Foreign Relations, p. 17. Also see Pacific Basin Economic Council, *PBEC Report: Sydney Meeting—1980* (publication details unknown), p. 27.
12. U.S., Congress, House, Subcommittee on Asian and Pacific Affairs, *Hearings: The Pacific Community Idea*, 96th Cong., 1st Sess., 1979, p. iii.
13. Also see Sir John Crawford, "Pacific Community Seminar: Chairman's Background Notes," unpublished personal notes.
14. Kolde.
15. Harlan Cleveland and Michael Hirschfeld, *The Pacific Basin Project: Prospectus of a Two-Year Work Program, 1980-81*, a report prepared by the Aspen Institute for Humanistic Studies: Program in International Affairs (Princeton, n.d.). Also see U.S., Congress, Senate, Committee on Foreign Relations, p. 19.
16. George Chaplin and Glenn D. Paige, eds., *Hawaii 2000: Continuing Experiment in Anticipatory Democracy* (Honolulu, 1973), pp. 334-355.
17. George S. Kanahele and Michael Haas, "Prospects for a Pacific Community," *Pacific Community*, 6, no. 1 (October 1974): 83-93.
18. Memorandum from Michael Haas to Pacific Council Organizers, April 7, 1975 (in the files of George S. Kanahele).

Introduction

19. Ato Masuda, *The Pacific Council of Japan* (Tokyo, 1975). Also see letter from Masuda to Kanahele, July 18, 1980, in the files of George S. Kanahele.
20. See *Honolulu Advertiser*, August 10-14, 1980, for an excellent example of current newspaper reporting.
21. Robert H. Hewett, ed., *Future Economic and Security Cooperation in the Pacific Region: A Private Conference of the Pacific Forum* (Honolulu, 1979), back cover.
22. John Edwards, "Moulding a New Community," *Far Eastern Economic Review*, August 22, 1980. Also see *Honolulu Advertiser*, June 21, 1980.
23. "Pacific Telecommunications Council Established," statement prepared by staff, Honolulu, January 9, 1980, in the files of the Council.
24. Derek Davies, "Exploiting the Pacific Tide," *Far Eastern Economic Review*, December 21, 1979.
25. Ibid., pp. 48-52.
26. Helen Ester, "Slow Start in the Pacific," *Far Eastern Economic Review*, September 26, 1980. Also see Crawford.
27. See *North-South: A Program for Survival—The Brandt Commission Report* (Cambridge, Mass., 1980); and summary comments on the Mitsubishi report in "The Dangerous Imbalance," *World Press Review*, March 1980.
28. For example, see *Washington Post*, September 1, 1980.
29. *New York Times*, August 31, 1980.
30. *Honolulu Advertiser*, August 26, 1980.
31. U.S., Congress, House, Subcommittee on Asian and Pacific Affairs, pp. 106-108.
32. U.S., Congress, Senate, Committee on Foreign Relations, pp. 26-27.
33. Ibid., pp. 13-17.
34. Pacific Basin Economic Council, p. 3.
35. U.S., Congress, Senate, Committee on Foreign Relations, p. 16.
36. Davies, pp. 48-50.
37. See *The Future of International Governance: Prospectus for a New, and Different, Inquiry*, a report prepared by the Aspen Institute for Humanistic Studies: Program in International Affairs (Princeton: December 13, 1979), pp. 1-3.

Economic Cooperation in a Pacific Community

Kiyoshi Kojima

May 22, 1980

Kiyoshi Kojima, an internationally acclaimed economist from Hitotsubashi University, has been writing and speaking about the prospects for forging a regional community in the Pacific since the early 1960s. His address in this series is a summary of his views as they have evolved over the years since. After reviewing the history of the movement and evaluating the several available models for future institutional structuring, he concludes that the Organization for Pacific Trade and Development concept as discussed in the Patrick-Drysdale proposal is the most appropriate basis for action. It is, he argues, the structure most capable of facilitating the development of the region's economic potential while remaining responsive to such political realities as the presence of the Association of South East Asian Nations, the necessity of developmental aid for certain nations, and the general importance of promoting joint-venture industrial development. Professor Kojima, doubtlessly the world's most prolific author on the notion of community in the Pacific, is often cited as one of the founding fathers of the concept.

As we are all aware, 1980 is the twentieth anniversary of the East-West Center, and the Pacific Community Lecture Series is one of several special programs designed to celebrate the occasion. Hence, it is a great honor for me to be here and to participate in the celebration as a speaker in this series.

There are several more specific reasons why I am particularly pleased to be part of this program. In the first instance, I am sometimes credited with being one of the founding fathers of the Pacific community concept, and the East-West Center is at least partially responsible for this being so. In February 1964 the Center sponsored a conference entitled "Economic Cooperation for Development and Trade in the Pacific," and it was at this gathering that the concept was first discussed and thought through. Fascinated by the possibilities, I have since been actively involved with the effort to transform theory into action. Therefore, I am pleased to return to the Center—the place where it all began for me—to further develop my thoughts on building a Pacific community. Secondly, and on an even more personal note, I am also happy to be here at this particular time as today is my sixtieth birthday and, hence, *Kan-Reki*, which in the Orient means a fresh, second round of life.

Against this auspicious background, please join me in an exploration of economic cooperation in a Pacific community, some of the past problems and some of the future prospects.

Pacific Trade and Development Conferences

In November 1965, still very much excited by the East-West Center conference, I presented a paper entitled "A Pacific Economic Community and Asian Developing Countries" to the Japan Economic Research Center Conference. As a result of this presentation, Mr. Takeo Miki, then Japan's foreign minister, asked that I travel through the Pacific rim countries—including Hawaii—surveying the degree of interest in the idea of a Pacific economic community. I spent two months early in 1967 at this task.

Inspired by the interest I detected in this survey, I, with the support of Foreign Minister Miki, called a Pacific Trade and Development Conference (PAFTAD) during January 1968 in Tokyo. It was a success, and a second one was held at the East-West Center in January 1969. At that time I proposed the establishment of a Pacific Free Trade Area based upon the five advanced countries of the Pacific (the United States, Canada, Japan, Australia, and New Zealand) with the developing nations of the region as associate members. The success of the initial conferences led to still further gatherings and so it is that the PAFTAD conferences are now recognized as important events in Pacific Basin affairs. The tenth conference, "ASEAN in a Changing Pacific and World Economy," was held in Canberra, Australia during March 1979, and the eleventh conference is scheduled for Seoul, South Korea in September 1980.

Participants in the various PAFTAD conferences have largely been policy-oriented academic and business economists, government leaders, and central bank officials (all acting in a private capacity) from throughout the Pacific region. Among the key individuals over the years have been Professor Hugh Patrick, the late Professor Harry Johnson, and Dr. Larry Krause from the United States; Professor H. Edward English from Canada; Sir John Crawford and Dr. Peter Drysdale from Australia; and Dr. Saburo Okita and myself from Japan.

One of the best examples of the significance of these gatherings, especially their encouragement of joint research studies, came in 1978 when Professor Patrick and Dr. Drysdale were asked by the Subcommittee on East Asian and Pacific Affairs of the United States Senate's Committee on Foreign Relations to study the question of Pacific economic regionalism. Their report, entitled *An Asian-Pacific Regional Economic Organization: An Exploratory Concept Paper* and issued by the subcommittee in July 1979, advocates the creation of an "Organization for Pacific Trade and Development" (OPTAD) to enhance trade, development, and resource use planning throughout the Pacific. This, at least in my opinion, is one of the most authoritative papers on a Pacific economic community published so far. Basically I share their view on the necessity of such an organization, although I have minor reservations with respect to membership and the assignment of task forces. Indeed, I myself recently published a similar paper entitled, like this speech, "Economic Cooperation in a Pacific Community."

The Concept of a Pacific Community

We may conceive of three basic concepts of a Pacific community, each unique as a result of different areas of concern and different degrees of integration.

The first concept involves a high degree of institutional integration, such as the European Economic Community, and is based upon a customs union or, to use a name once common, a Pacific Free Trade Area, a possibility that I once advocated. A free trade zone with restrictions against nonmembers is not now feasible largely because it is inconsistent with the commitment of the United States and Japan to an open, multilateral, global economic system. Further, since the General Agreement on Tariffs and

Trade has been successful in reducing tariffs and other trade barriers throughout the world, a free trade area in the Pacific is no longer of any great value.

The second concept involves a much broader area of concern and reduced degree of integration. As Dr. Everett Kleinjans, president of the East-West Center, stated in recent testimony before the House Subcommittee on Asian and Pacific Affairs, "it [this concept of a Pacific community] indicates friendly relationships among persons and institutions of different nations; it means cooperative research ventures in the various scientific, social scientific, and humanistic disciplines on problems of mutual concern; it means enlightened communication beyond racial, national, or cultural boundaries. Certain shared values, perceptions, beliefs, and behavior are necessary to improve communication and cooperation."

Similar views are expressed in a recent Japanese report. Prime Minister Masayoshi Ohira, keen to promote the building of a Pacific community, created a Pacific Basin Cooperation Study Group following his election in 1978, and this group recently issued a document entitled *Interim Report on the Pacific Basin Cooperation Concept*. This report, ranking with the United States Senate's OPTAD proposal as an important and authoritative document, observes that: "The Pacific Basin Cooperation Concept, which we espouse here, is intended . . . to promote cooperative relations within the Pacific basin region and to take maximum advantage of the area's rich potential not only for the Pacific basin countries but also to enhance the prosperity and well-being of all peoples in the world." It goes on to suggest expanded exchanges in the social and cultural fields to enhance mutual understanding, greater mutual efforts in scientific and technological research, and various new modes of economic cooperation. It does not touch upon the question of regional cooperation in political and military matters.

This concept of the Pacific community is too broad, making the concept itself too vague and ambiguous and its objectives too diverse. The social and cultural bases for a Pacific community are indeed important and should not be neglected, but mutual understanding and interaction can be enhanced short of creating a Pacific Basin–wide framework. The effort to build a Pacific community should focus on a clear-cut objective, namely, the development of mechanisms for regional-multilateral cooperation in the efficient utilization of underdeveloped economic potential so as to further the peace and security of all the peoples in the region. These are the most urgent and common concerns in the uncertain world of the present.

Hence, a third concept is necessary, one that is institutionally less rigid than that underlying the European Economic Community but yet more precise than that behind the current Japanese proposal. It is increasingly evident to me that the Senate's OPTAD proposal is most appropriate in this respect. Although the precise nature of such an organization has yet to be defined, it would aim at fostering regional economic development by encouraging functional integration in several important aspects involving certain less rigid institutional frameworks, the members of which would vary according to the particular function. As Professor Patrick states, an "OPTAD would be a governmental organization with a small administrative apparatus so as not to become heavily bureaucratic, with specific Task Forces to handle defined policy-oriented assignments, and an informal, consultative, communicative style of operations." In short, it would provide a forum for consultation and cooperation among all the nations of the region, advanced and developing.

A New Development Center in the World Economy

The next step is to enquire as to why closer economic cooperation is necessary in a Pacific community; what kinds of cooperative measures are effective and what is their contribution; and what difficulties and obstacles hamper the realization of these measures.

What the world economy most needs in the coming decade is a new and large development center. Following the devaluation of the pound in 1949, the world economy in the 1950s recovered and surged forward as a result of such factors as the Marshall Plan in Europe, economic assistance to Japan, and the outbreak of the Korean war. Similarly, after recovering from the 1957 recession, the world economy enjoyed unprecedented expansion due to the formation and progress of the European Economic Community and the European Free Trade Association and the rapid growth of Japan's heavy and chemical industries.

This pattern did not repeat itself during the 1970s. No buoyant new forces appeared, and, further complicating matters, deadlocks were reached in many areas of the world economy. The international exchange-rate system, the liberalization of international trade, the North-South problem, and the energy crisis are examples. Thus, the 1970s have been a decade of continuing confusion and uncertainty. It is widely believed that this circumstance can be overcome only through the creation of a new and dynamic world developmental center and that the Pacific, with its great overall potential, may become that center. So it is that the twenty-first century is often termed the "Century of the Pacific."

The Pacific Basin, composed of the five advanced nations (United States, Japan, Canada, Australia, and New Zealand) and the numerous developing nations of Asia, Latin America, and Oceania, is a vast area with seemingly unlimited potential for economic development. In terms of population, in 1975 the total for the advanced countries was 365 million: 213 million in the United States, 112 million in Japan, 13 million in Australia, and 3 million in New Zealand. The Southeast Asian nations, led by Indonesia and followed by the Philippines, Thailand, Malaysia, and Singapore, accounted for 235 million. In East Asia, China accounted for more than 900 million, while South Korea, Taiwan, and Hong Kong added another 56 million to the total. The total in Latin America was approximately 275 million, while Oceania contributed another 4 million. Thus the overall population of the region was some 1 billion, 835 million, huge indeed when compared with Western Europe, the world's most recent great developmental center, with a total comparable population of approximately 259 million.

While Western Europe is more or less homogeneous and uniformly industrialized, the Pacific includes nations of very different political and cultural backgrounds as well as diverse economies. Some countries are well endowed with natural resources while others are poorly endowed. Some are economically too small and others too large, and nearly all are different in terms of levels of industrialization and national income. Yet, regardless of the difficulties these heterogeneities pose with respect to building a Pacific community, there is great potential for regional integration and, hence, economic development.

Many economists, including myself, believe that the rationality of economic theory and the progress of technology are neutral and universally applicable despite any diversities arising from such factors as cultural and political conditions, the size of the economy, and its stage of development. A basic principle in this belief is the theory of the international division of labor which holds that when one country gains an advantage in the specialized production and export of a particular commodity, it provides an opportunity for one of its trading partners to produce and export still another commodity to its own advantage, whatever the differences in size, stage of development, and demand between the nations. In short, the theory shows why trading nations are interdependent and, moreover, why they tend to be prosperous, both important incentives in the development of any regional economic community.

Interdependence is further encouraged by official aid and private direct investment which compensate for the lack of infrastructure, capital, technology, and management skills so often found in less-advanced economies. Low-cost production, which was not previously possible because of the lack of these elements, becomes feasible. Hence, based upon the new comparative costs, harmonious trade grows. Although there are sometimes exceptions in the case of official aid, direct foreign investment ought to be undertaken in accordance with comparative costs. If it is released from a comparatively disadvantageous industry in the investing country and finds its way into an industry with overt or potential comparative advantage in the host country, it will promote a harmonious upgrading of industrial structure on both sides and thus speed the expansion of trade between the two countries. This is what I call Japanese-type or trade-oriented direct foreign investment.

Through an appropriate intensification of official aid, direct investment, and trade liberalization (a subject that will be explored in more detail momentarily as it is the essence of economic cooperation in a Pacific community), the day will come when the per capita national income in the developing countries is equal to that in the advanced countries. However, until this happens—until developing countries have reached a standard of living equal to America's or Japan's and until we have created interdependent relationships close enough to be inseparable—we can never achieve lasting regional political and economic stability.

While the Pacific rim countries have considerable potential for growth of trade and development, they have lacked the leadership and initiative necessary to develop this potential. A sense of solidarity and a framework for economic cooperation have yet to emerge in the Pacific region. The United States has maintained a general attitude of "going in with Europe" and has tended to neglect the Pacific region. At the same time, Japan, remembering the nightmare of the Greater East Asian Co-Prosperity Sphere, has, at least until recently, hesitated to take any initiatives toward building a Pacific community.

The model that comes first to mind for achieving these ends is, of course, the European community. Active and adaptable leaders have, over the years, taken the initiative and built a prosperous community within Europe itself, and a broader Atlantic community involving both Europe and North America. The first major event in this process was the inauguration of the European Economic Community in 1958. Among subsequent highlights were the complete elimination of inner tariffs in 1968; the enlargement of the community to include the United Kingdom, Ireland, and Denmark in 1973; its further expansion by means of special arrangements with certain African, Caribbean, and Pacific nations under terms of the Lomé Treaty of 1975; and the inauguration of the European Monetary System in 1979. Although the successful growth of the European community has not been entirely a consequence of its institutional integration, such integration has been a major factor. This, as suggested earlier, may pose some problems so far as the Pacific is concerned.

In the same vein, the Organization for Economic Cooperation and Development, a group that evolved out of the Marshall Plan administration and now the principal group concerned with global economic cooperation, is sometimes cited as an organization that might be used to encourage greater cooperation in the Pacific. Appropriate as this suggestion may be in theory, in practice the group has retained its essential European-Atlantic orientation. Even after Japan, Australia, and New Zealand became participants, its membership remained largely European-Atlantic and its interests and policies have continued to be directed toward European-Atlantic problems. The interests and problems of the Pacific region, largely different in nature from those of the European-Atlantic region, have been neglected.

This bias is further evident in the five economic summit conferences convened by world leaders since 1975. Judging from the participants and topics of discussion, world concern remains fixed on Europe and the Atlantic regardless of the potential and the problems of the Pacific.

It seems to me that all of this leads to the conclusion that, valuable as the European experience may be as a general guide, we need our own unique forum in the Pacific to discuss political, cultural, and economic issues common to the region, and that the oft-mentioned OPTAD proposal comes closest to meeting this need. By now Australia, Canada, and New Zealand, turning their eyes away from the mother country and Europe, are keenly interested in peace and prosperity in the Pacific region. Notwithstanding the continued difficulties, industrialization in developing nations has been under way at a rapid tempo, especially in the Asian-Pacific nations. South Korea, Taiwan, Hong Kong, and Singapore have developed into newly industrializing countries, and the other Association for South East Asian Nations (ASEAN) countries will reach a similar stage in the not-too-distant future. Additionally, China has begun the modernization of her huge economy. Thus, both the five advanced countries and the developing nations of the Pacific are keen to take the initiative in establishing some kind of policy forum for economic cooperation among themselves.

Starting with an ASEAN-Pacific Forum

It would be premature and difficult at this time to define the formal membership of an OPTAD. It would be preferable to foster functional, rather than institutional, integration in the region by employing a problem-by-problem approach towards economic development and trade growth among the countries of the area. Moreover, since the numerous Pacific rim countries cover a large area and are heterogeneous in size and nature, it would, at least at the outset, be more realistic to make an approach towards subregional issues rather than towards the complex affairs of the entire Pacific region.

Of the various practical tasks that an OPTAD might undertake, it seems to me that the most urgent issue is the successful resolution of the North-South (the rich nation–poor nation) problem in the Pacific region. Efforts to resolve this dilemma on a global basis within the framework of such organizations as the United Nations Conference on Trade and Development and the United Nations Industrial Development Organization have proved unrealistic and fruitless. The differences among the various regional groups—the Asian group as opposed to the African group is a case in point—simply have been too great to permit any workable agreements. The lesson, I think, is clear. Only those nations that have an intimate knowledge of the particular regional and subregional economic issues are able to contribute to effective solutions, and this kind of a grouping can most suitably be arranged by an OPTAD.

While it is clear that all the various nations of the region stand to profit from the formation of an OPTAD, it is less clear just how organizational efforts should proceed. The five advanced nations might be expected to take the initiative, but that could prove intimidating to some of the likely participants. A desirable alternative would be for ASEAN, a group with considerable stake in any such venture, to take the initiative and establish an ASEAN-Pacific forum, a subregional OPTAD involving the ASEAN nations and the five advanced Pacific nations. Once operational, it could invite the participation of the other nations of the region, eventually transforming itself into a fully regional organization. Should, on the other hand, the creation of a single, region-wide organization somehow prove to be too difficult a task, a series of separate, subregional groups, each with the five advanced nations as members, could be formed. Thus, there could be an East Asia–Pacific forum, a Pacific Islands–Pacific forum, and even a Latin American–Pacific forum to complement the ASEAN-Pacific forum. Although it would be desirable for China to participate in the East Asia–Pacific forum, the possibility of organizing still another forum—the China-Pacific forum—could be considered should it prove advisable. Indirect as it might be, such an arrangement would still produce joint policy.

Using the ASEAN-Pacific forum as an example, I would like to sketch out how economic development and trade growth in the ASEAN nations would be accelerated. The primary target of such an organization would be to raise the levels of the ASEAN economies rapidly and efficiently through aid and direct investment from the advanced Pacific countries and through the opening of wider markets for their products. In the final phase, the present ASEAN economies should have grown to an industrialized stage equivalent to that of the advanced Pacific countries and thus forged an interdependent and equal relationship with the advanced nations similar to that of present-day Europe.

Thus far all the advanced Pacific countries have insisted upon a bilateral approach with the ASEAN nations in providing official aid, making direct investments, and arranging trade preferences. However, if a regional-multilateral approach such as advocated here were to be put into effect, a larger and more efficient contribution to economic development and trade growth for all parties could be anticipated. Equally important, the danger of over-presence and domination by one or another of the advanced nations, ever present under existing bilateral relationships, would be avoided. In addition, as the following suggestions illustrate, a number of more specific benefits might also be realized:

1. Official development aid to the area could be pooled and used in a multilateral, no-strings fashion through the creation of a revolving aid fund. Annual aid commitments from the five advanced Pacific countries could be deposited with the Asian Development Bank to establish the fund. The scheme could be applied to official bilateral aid, including technical assistance, sales in receipt of local currency, and official export credits. Without requiring additional annual aid commitments, the scheme could be made operational immediately. The object would be to work towards the removal of strings from bilateral aid to Southeast Asian countries.

    The revolving aid fund scheme involves the acceptance of two important principles. The first is that aid credited to the fund would have to be completely unfettered so far as procurements are concerned (i.e., procurements could be made in any donor country or any ASEAN country). The second is that any positive imbalance between a country's sales under aid procurements and its aid commitment should be held with the fund. The original deposits and accumulated deposits could not be withdrawn from the fund, but would be utilized by aid receivers in subsequent years. To illustrate, suppose that donor country

A provides $500 million worth of aid but only $400 million is spent, while donor country B provides $500 million but exports goods and services to the value of $600 million to the recipient countries. Country B would accumulate a $100 million credit with the fund, raising its total to $600 million, while country A's total would decline commensurately. Thus country B would have automatically increased its aid commitments by $100 million in the second year. Had the freeing of this aid taken place outside the fund, country B would have earned foreign exchange at country A's expense. The revolving aid fund obviates this exchange problem essentially because it requires that country B's aid obligation increase automatically with excess earnings. The end result is that the effectiveness of the total aid program would increase even though the amounts involved remained unchanged.

The revolving aid fund scheme could be used for several other important purposes, since deposits would accumulate over time from the gap between annual aid commitments and disbursements (usually some 20 to 30 percent), and from deposits by excess exporters. Let me suggest four possibilities:

a. ASEAN countries could be assisted in their economic development through a stabilization of export earnings (STABEX) scheme for certain primary products. Loans for compensation of export income losses, with very low interest rates, could be provided from the fund.
b. Subregional buffer stocks in rice, timber, and other products in which ASEAN countries have intense and common interests could be created in order to stabilize prices and export earnings relative to those products. The revolving aid fund could provide loans to establish buffer stock schemes when appropriate.
c. It is important to stimulate the development of natural resources in the Pacific region. The revolving aid fund could be used to supply low-interest loans for research and the exploration for mineral resources, and also to provide international insurance coverage for private foreign investment.
d. ASEAN exporters require access to funds for export

credit in order to provide terms which are competitive with those of exporters in advanced countries. The ability to provide export credit to buyers, within and outside the region, will become more important as the capacity for industrial exports grows. The revolving aid fund could be used to provide export credit funds for the benefit of Southeast Asian countries.

Perhaps I have dwelt too much upon technicalities relative to the revolving aid fund scheme, but the fact is that, if coordinated policy actions are taken, there is room to facilitate massive subregional economic development through such a device.

The other major benefits of an ASEAN-Pacific forum can be cited more briefly:

2. Official development aid from the Pacific advanced countries to the ASEAN nations could be greatly enlarged. The aid should cover many projects, including ASEAN complementary industries which have already been planned. In addition, new large-scale aid directed at such ends as doubling rice production and constructing an ocean-transportation network, ought to be considered.
3. Joint venture investments and non-equity arrangements between advanced countries and ASEAN countries could be encouraged for the development of mineral and other natural resources, for the establishment of light consumer manufacturing, and for the creation of heavy industrial growth points (including ASEAN complementary industries). In all instances the projects should be economically efficient and competitive.
4. In order to improve market access for ASEAN products—both primary products and manufactures—advanced countries have provided generalized preferences on more generous terms and have reduced most-favored-nation tariffs through the General Agreement on Tariffs and Trade negotiations. These efforts have not been sufficient and must be much improved despite the fact that counteractions, such as the strengthening of safeguard clauses, have recently appeared. In addition, structural adjustment in developed countries must be undertaken to nurture and en-

courage the expansion of ASEAN trade which will come in response to the boomerang effects of past aid and investment. Advanced countries must cooperate with respect to preferences and structural adjustment. If only one country establishes an open market policy, reduces tariffs, and undertakes preferences and structural adjustment, the export products from the developing economies would be directed at that country, thereby causing a deterioration in its international balance of payments and in its level of employment. It is essential that all advanced countries cooperate in adopting at least vaguely similar open market policies. Common considerations on value-added tariffs and cumulative ASEAN contents should be given attention. A cooperative policy is as essential here as it is in the case of domestic demand management and business recovery policy among advanced countries. It goes without saying that an ASEAN-Pacific forum would provide the concerned nations with an avenue for dialogue on these matters.

Pacific Region-wide Cooperation

In addition to subregional economic development, there are a number of more general, region-wide functions that an extended ASEAN-Pacific forum or more broadly based OPTAD might perform. Some of the more important are as follows:

1. It is essential that the exchange of social and cultural knowledge be promoted in order to enhance mutual understanding among the diverse nations in the Pacific region and to create a basis for regional solidarity. An intensification of exchanges in the areas of at least research, education, and personnel is necessary.
2. Technological progress in transportation and communication has already facilitated increased regional exchanges in the areas of culture, personnel, products, and investment. Still further developments, including an increase in tourism, are awaited with the hope that expanded volume will lower costs.
3. The Pacific has a great potential for the development of marine resources, including fishing and seabed mining. De-

velopment in this area must, however, be undertaken with discipline and within a region-wide cooperative framework involving all the nations concerned.
4. It is important that efforts be made to secure adequate food supplies and to stabilize food prices throughout the Pacific Basin.
5. It is also important that secure, safe energy bases be established in the Pacific region. This involves such controversial matters as creating a regional joint oil stock, constructing an oil relay base, developing oil resources in the region, funding research on the commercial production of alternative energy sources, and building a regional nuclear energy recycling system.
6. Similar efforts must be made to assure the availability of other natural resources in the Pacific Basin region.
7. All nations involved in these activities must pay appropriate heed to questions of environmental protection.

The list of concerns common to all the Pacific rim countries could go on endlessly. The point, however, is already clear. All these concerns have region-wide rather than simply national implications and their solutions are more likely to be found in region-wide efforts. We must, therefore, intensify our efforts in that direction.

A Campaign for the Age of the Pacific

Both the more urgent task of facilitating subregional economic development and the more general aim of building an infrastructure connecting the entire Pacific Basin region may, in due time, become strong motivations for establishing new institutions in the region. At this stage, however, a sense of great hesitancy seems to prevail in most countries around the Pacific, and no consensus has developed with respect to the establishment of an OPTAD or any other form of a Pacific community.

As a consequence, what we need to do now is launch a campaign for the "age of the Pacific." We need to convene as many conferences, symposiums, and seminars as possible at all levels of academia, business, and government. In this fashion we can best direct attention to the development potential and the need for cooperation in the Pacific region. Against this background, the East-West Center's present activities are most welcome. An international symposium on Pacific Basin cooperation [the Pacific Community Seminar] will be held in Canberra during the coming autumn. Still other conferences and projects are planned by various nations and organizations from the region. All of these will contribute to a campaign for the age of the Pacific and, of course, to improved ideas and the eventual emergence of a consensus.

In the meantime, international task forces or research institutes should be established immediately to study the various problems discussed in this paper. They must be truly international—with participation from the developing nations, China, and the Soviet Union as well as the advanced Pacific countries—although participation will of course vary with the issues discussed. Hawaii may be among the most suitable locations for a research institution dealing with social and cultural issues in the Pacific region. Further, I am hoping—as the chairman of the Pacific Trade and Development Conference—that the conference will be remodelled into a research institution on Pacific trade and economic development with a permanent office and research facilities in, say, Canberra and with annual conferences held at various locations around the Pacific. I also hope that the leaders of the five advanced Pacific countries and the other Pacific rim nations can hold a subsummit gathering to develop at least certain common views on economics prior to the Venetian summit conference in June.

Mr. President, ladies and gentlemen: I thank you for inviting me this evening to speak on this interesting and important topic.

Building a Pacific Community
Ratu Kamisese K. T. Mara
March 26 and June 11, 1980

Ratu Mara, the prime minister of Fiji, is one of the recognized elder statesmen of Oceania. Hence, his lecture series address—actually a synthesis of two separate talks on Pacific issues delivered at the East-West Center—has attracted special attention. This is fortunate as the talk contains some of the most provocative—there are those who would say "contrary"—remarks delivered over the course of the series. Briefly stated, he offers a rousing defense of traditional Pacific Island culture and questions the wisdom of any wholesale adaptation of modern techniques such as those envisioned by most Pacific community advocates. Further, he wonders aloud whether or not the regionalist movement will, in effect, serve to reintroduce colonial controls over the island nations of the area. He concludes with a powerful plea for a much greater degree of pluralism and decentralism in any new regional arrangement than most of the other advocates appear willing to accept.

I am very pleased to have been invited to speak in this very important series. I welcome such an opportunity. It shows that the East-West Center, situated as it is in the Pacific, is nevertheless conscious that it could perhaps do more for the Pacific and in particular the smaller Pacific Islands. It is, after all, a center, and a center must retain its equilibrium. It will only do this as it balances the attention and study it is prepared to give to both the East and West.

Not only have you been ready to mount a series of this kind, but you have had the courtesy (modesty forbids me from saying the good sense) to invite participation from those who are most affected. There is a plethora of experts these days, mostly from the outside looking in. It is therefore refreshing to see a realization that those actually located in the environment and imbued with its traditions and cultures have a contribution, and perhaps a major contribution, to make to such studies. This is not to decry the help and advice that can be given by an external impartial adviser, particularly if he is of the sympathetic kind, but the starting point surely must be the people of the region themselves.

In fact, particularly when it comes to identifying the problems, who knows better than the owner where the shoe pinches? It is, rather, when it comes to repairing the shoe that there can perhaps be a place for the expert. In the same way, in the professional field, it has been said that the man who is his own lawyer has a fool for a client; but in that sphere too, it is the man himself who knows what is his complaint.

Hence my being with you today is an attempt to focus on the issue through Pacific eyes.

I am sure you will forgive me if I start, not only from Fiji, but indeed from my own home on the island of Lakeba, the seat of the high chiefs of Lau. Recent archaeological excavations in Lakeba have uncovered the remains of a man of about thirty to thirty-five which have been dated about 500 B.C.—prior to the age of Pericles and Athens' Golden Age. These remains were closely associated with some fragments of pottery which are in style a variety of the form archaeologists call Lapita. Similar pottery has been found from New Britain across the Pacific as far east as Samoa. And this, in its turn, gives support to the theory that the makers of this pottery in the eastern Pacific regions were the ancestral Polynesians. It is even possible that at that stage they flourished initially in the Fiji group. However that may be, these findings seem to discredit some of the complicated stories of Polynesian origins out of mainland Asia or, even more farfetched, from the Middle East or Africa.

"Always something new out of Africa," the well-known tag declares, but *not* the Polynesians.

There was, then, in the fifth century before Christ, a society at Lakeba with its own culture and way of life. That society has survived to this day, receiving and assimilating cultures and waves of immigrants (although assimilation should not be taken too literally in dealing with this part of Fiji). Recent researches by Professor Brookfield and Mr. A. C. Reid have revealed a well-developed society with a political and administrative machinery functioning well and effectively.

Previously our history and cultural traditions had depended heavily for their recording and transmission on the works of early missionary writers. It is now becoming apparent that such accounts should be regarded with grave skepticism. Their writers had an axe to grind, and they were able to use all the weight of monopoly historians to press their case. They portray the coming of the missionaries purely as an altruistic and evangelical venture. This is to ignore and discount the efforts of the leaders of these peoples themselves to bring missionaries to their land, of which more in a moment. They portray the indigenous people as a primitive and backward race whose only salvation in this world was the Bible and in the consumer goods supplied by the commercial traders following in their train. All this was written of a society with a long historical development of culture and way of life which had inhabited this world for two and a half thousand years.

I promised to say a little more about the coming of Christianity to Lakeba. It was about 1826 that Malani, the high chief of Lau, hearing reports of Christianity in the Pacific, decided to send one Takai to find out more and report back. Takai himself was a fascinating character whose story will be published in due course by Mr. Reid. Suffice it to say that his origins were from Tonga, from Vanua Levu, and from Lau. This gave him the clue for his first port of call to find the Christian message—Tonga, where a Reverend Mr. Lawrie was engaged in disseminating the Methodist Gospel. From there he took steps with Dillon, a staunch Catholic. After the lapse of a couple of years and journeys that took him to the New Hebrides, Sydney, and Tahiti, he eventually landed again in Lakeba with two volunteer Tahitian missionaries with the London Missionary Society imprint. Takai sounds very like the first ecumenical in the Pacific—so much so, that a churchman of a certain denomination said of Takai in a brief but pithy obituary, "he died, *I hope*, in the Christian faith." A slightly skeptical epitaph.

Now here the story takes an interesting turn and a new relevance to our theme. Malani, while professing interest in the missionaries, was not prepared to receive them on his own initiative and first had to call a council of his island leaders for discussion. Pending this, the missionaries could take off for Oneata. So here is a well-established consultative machinery which is involved at times of decision. At the end of the day the decision is announced in the name of the chief, but its formulation is by consensus. I shall have more to say of this also in relation to administration of communities.

It was not so long ago that I had a personal experience of the sort where we in the Pacific could perhaps find our own solutions were it not for the imposition of other concepts and values and, indeed, of language. You are probably aware that, at the invitation of the Gilbert Islands government and Rabi Council of Leaders, I have been endeavoring to help find a solution to what is a very difficult, but nevertheless very real problem in the Pacific. To a large extent the arguments seem to hinge on sovereignty and ownership, and yet these are words which have no parallel in our Pacific society. One of the very first things we had to do was to sit down and try to set out in simple and Pacific terms what exactly were the intentions, claims, and proposals of those concerned. It was surprising that, once this had been done, there was at least some measure of agreement on what should be the next step, whereas previously it had been doubtful whether there would be a next step at all. At the same time we found that the presence of advisers on both sides, even though I had rigidly excluded them from the actual meetings, tended to impose on their associates an inflexibility and almost a hostility which were foreign to the personalities and traditional characters of the people themselves.

This may seem a rather long introduction for a keynote address for a talk entitled "Building a Pacific Community," but what it is basically trying to show is that there is a Pacific community already, and that it has been there—or should I say "here"?—for at least two and a half thousand years. Not only was it a community, but it was an organized and specialized community. There were specialists (I hesitate to brand them as experts) in religion, housebuilding, agriculture, navigation, the arts, etc.

We should not be trying to build a Pacific community; we should be trying to build *upon* a Pacific community which is already in existence. Even in the wider context of relationships between Pacific states, I remember a remark I made after one of the early Pacific Forum meetings. I said that we were not so much establishing new friendships as renewing old ancestral ties which the arbitrary division of the metropolitan powers in the Pacific had weakened. What has been wrong with development planning in the Pacific has been that all this has been largely disregarded. Development planning has been done on the basis that there were no real, viable societies.

Such development planning should not only take account of specialized skills already existing in the society, but also give needed encouragement and support. In addition, it should look to traditional knowledge as to when and what should be done. The preacher of Ecclesiastes says, "for everything there is a season, and a time for every matter under heaven." He begins by saying "A time to be born and a time to die," and perhaps there is not too much we can do about that, though the advance of medical science constantly surprises us. But then he goes on to say, "A time to plant, and a time to pluck up that which is planted." In this the Pacific has a traditional wisdom and experience.

We hear so much these days of agricultural science, and we immediately think of test tubes, laboratories, fertilizers, weedicides, new technology and equipment. We forget that science really means knowledge—including applied knowledge. There is a place for modern techniques, but as complementary to, and not in substitution for, traditional knowledge and the traditional application of it.

The corpus of the Pacific's agricultural knowledge must go back a very long way. It evolved over ages and was passed down by word and example from father to son. It must have been built up by trial and error, by astute observation, by selection of the most successful varieties, and by the development of appropriate agricultural practices. It was a system whereby the old farmers were able to assure themselves of an adequate food supply in various forms. At the same time it was a method of preserving the carbohydrate foods (dalo, breadfruit, vudi) in pits, enabling the people to survive droughts, hurricanes, wars, and other calamities. Yams were, of course, a ready-made crop for preservation.

One has only to look at the names of the old Fijian calendar to see how life revolved around planting and fishing, and also how experience over the years had given people the knowledge of the right season of the year for the various operations. These names also stressed the importance of yam cultivation. The year was divided into eleven months, and the only months not bearing names indicative of yam cultivation were those during which the crop required no particular attention or had been safely housed.

It may have been that the old planters could not give complete explanations as to why they planted, weeded, harvested, and did whatever else they had to do. But they did know that if they followed certain natural indicators they could not go wrong. All these indicators are still with us today, but they probably do not form part of an agricultural syllabus. It may be that modern agricultural science considers these too old-fashioned. But there are lessons to be learned that have been forgotten in the march of progress. One has only to look at the new-found interest in traditional medicinal plants and the intense re-examination that is being conducted. I think I raised this subject at the South Pacific Commission close on fifteen years ago and only recently have we begun to get results.

One hears that research is being conducted into varieties of yams, dalo, kumala, duruka, etc. Quite often, this work could be simplified and made more productive and economical if those doing the investigations took the trouble to find out from the old people how they use these things. In the process of finding out, much can be learned of the reasons certain varieties are preferred in different areas. Usually there are very good explanations (and scientifically based when worked out) relative to soil, or climate, or topography, or palatability, and so on. But researching varieties of dalo or yams that have twice the yield of the present ones loses much of its justification if no one will eat them.

The implication of all this is that agricultural practice, if successful in producing food consistently over the years, as the practice of the old farmers has been, is scientifically correct. The science of the system was built up on accumulated observation and practical experience. For the people of the time, explanations were obtained from natural (and sometimes supernatural) phenomena. As modern science has added new information and interpretations, different rationales have become accepted. But this has not invalidated practice as it existed previously; it has merely given it a different explanation. So again let us build on what we have, and let development plans do likewise.

I have discussed this at some length for several reasons. The first is to show that throughout the traditional agricultural and marine year activities were not carried on in a haphazard way, but in what I maintain was a scientific way in accordance with my earlier definition of science. The second reason is to illustrate the related but more basic point that there are still great differences between the outlook of the advanced industrial world and that of the Pacific Islands, and, at least for many of us in the Pacific, that the former is not ipso facto preferable to the latter.

Despite all the current talk of interdependence and the incommutable fact that much of the industrial world is indeed bound together by a web of interdependencies, many of the Pacific Island nations can still opt for self-sufficiency if they wish. It is still a viable option. The material standards of living may have to remain lower than in other parts of the world, but that may not be too high a price to pay for avoiding oil crises that tear at a society's very fabric, ruinous rates of inflation, crash programs of socioeconomic reform, and all the tensions that come with such events. The land and the sea can provide the basic needs of food, clothing, and shelter—and with them a good degree of satisfaction with life—and the debilitating traumas so common elsewhere can thus be avoided. All of this is well illustrated, although in a negative way, by New Zealand, one of our Pacific Island nations. It is a nation that can provide all the food it needs. It can grow potatoes, it can grow wheat, it can grow beef, it can grow lamb, and its seas abound with fish. Yet it is part of the international trading network in agricultural goods—that is to say it is interdependent—and it is consistently beset by economic problems, among them the highest rate of inflation of all the nations within our group.

Having made these observations, I do want to add the qualification that I am not in any way advocating a policy of total isolation for the Pacific Islands. The Pacific way, at least in my view, is founded first and foremost upon realism, and it is not realistic to believe, or even hope, that people in any part of the world can divorce themselves from other people elsewhere. There must and will be contact, and there must and will be sharing.

An illustrative case in point occurred during a recent visit to Japan. I was observing the cultivation of rice and pondering the advantages of that crop with respect to the fact that surpluses can safely be stored over extended periods of time, when I was informed that it was a relatively new aspect of Japanese agriculture, borrowed from still another culture. I began to wonder, then, whether or not it might be to Fiji's advantage to likewise adopt the crop. Rice, like the traditional taro, cassava, and yam, is suitable to our climate but, unlike the traditional crops which must be used shortly after harvesting, can also be stored for use during times when other crops are in short supply. Hence, by borrowing certain techniques, we can increase our ability to be self-sufficient. In other words, the self-sufficient policy I advocate is really a pluralistic policy—something Fiji understands well, given the composition of our society—wherein the old and the new, the traditional and the modern, exist side by side, enriching each other but never dominating each other. Such a symbiosis is possible—our experience proves it—and it is a part of the Pacific way. Hence, while I remain skeptical of much of the current talk of interdependence, especially so with respect to its ramifications for many of the Pacific Island nations, I seek no absolute disassociation from peoples and nations elsewhere throughout the region and the world. As long as the concept of cultural pluralism is observed and respected, there is a basis for bringing the Pacific closer together as a community.

When it comes to building a Pacific community in the more specific administrative sense, there is great room for experiment, but I suggest that the experiment of a colonial type of administration is neither best suited for such communities, nor does it take advantage of the built-in, traditional framework of communication and command.

So perhaps the first innovation worth trying is, paradoxically enough, a reversion to the precolonial system as it worked in the Pacific. This involved in many cases a small island with an almost completely autonomous self-governing unit which nevertheless owed its allegiance to a paramount center elsewhere. This seems to me a better alternative than carrying on the government from the center using a highly sophisticated administrative machinery involving a chain of command through commissioners, district officers, etc. Quite apart from the costly and perhaps impersonal nature of such a system, it bypasses the traditional sources of authority in social, economic, and cultural matters.

And I think it is in conformity with current trends of thought to decentralize and have smaller groups with a great measure of independence "doing their own thing." As I said earlier, these communities know their problems and they know their needs. Sometimes they will work out the solutions and will succeed on their own. At other times they will work out the solution but require some assistance to implement it. There may even be times when the problems seem to them insoluble, and that is the time when expert advice and assistance—if sought—makes sense.

But the progression I have outlined seems to me the right one. It retains the people's self-respect, it encourages them to develop their own initiative to the full, and ultimately it gives them the supreme satisfaction that they have been intimately involved and that they contributed to the limits of their capacity. From the perspective of the Pacific Island nations, at least, this is a workable model—perhaps the only workable model—for new regional initiatives, as, quite frankly, we fear the more centralized designs.

I alluded to the basis of our fear of the more centralized designs a moment ago in my reference to colonialism. Quite simply, we worry that the present interest in building a Pacific community, largely initiated by the big powers of the Pacific rim, could produce a web of new institutions and procedures having the practical—if not intended—effect of re-establishing a de facto form of colonial control over the smaller and more traditional nations of the region. Strange as this worry may sound in this day and age, it is nonetheless real in certain quarters and must, therefore, be expressed.

To illustrate, sometimes critics of my leadership in Fiji say "Look at the native Fijians: they lag behind the Indians, the Europeans, and the Chinese." I respond by saying "Look at the Maoris in New Zealand, look at the Malays in Malaysia, look at all the indigenous people of the smaller Pacific nations in relationship to the newcomers from elsewhere—they are not up to it when it comes to modern economic competition." And this is no abstraction. We see it at one level when we walk into a shop and there is one culture on one side of the counter with another culture on the other side of the counter. We see it at another level when we go to the South Pacific Commission or South Pacific Forum meetings and the big power members tell us we should not worry about the cost of certain desirable programs as they—the big powers—will assume the burden. They do, of course, but they also manage to put their people in the administrative positions with respect to those programs, and, in the end, policy is executed in accordance with their wishes rather than ours. Once again, one culture is on one side of the counter and another culture is on the other side.

Regrettably, none of the current proposals for institutionalizing the Pacific community concept that I have seen—including

Professor Kojima's suggestions for a series of subregional organizations based upon the ASEAN model—hold forth much prospect for resolving this very basic dilemma. They all call for a rather abrupt shift to a new but nonetheless essentially industrial economic order where, we fear, industrial civilization will dominate the smaller and more traditional societies of the Pacific Islands. We have only recently been weaned away from colonialism and paternalism, and we are anxious to avoid being caught up in something that might bring even vaguely similar circumstances back to the fore.

As a consequence, most of us from the Pacific Islands are going to respond to initiatives on this front with extreme caution. While we are pleased to participate in such limited ventures as the recent conference entitled "Development the Pacific Way" at the East-West Center, we are not, for example, participating in the more ambitious conference on the Pacific community scheduled at the Australian National University later this year. At this stage we need first to do our own thinking with respect to the regionalist concept and are not ready to participate in anything save the most decentralized undertakings lest the opportunity for consultation among ourselves be lost.

Having expressed these worries and doubts about the current regionalist movement with what I hope is sufficient clarity and force, let me once again reiterate my earlier statement to the effect that my comments should not be interpreted as a declaration of separation from the rest of the world. They are, on the contrary, only an attempt to illustrate some of the concerns that the smaller and more traditional nations of the Pacific are experiencing as they observe developments on the regionalist front.

In fact, despite our reservations, we recognize the need for greater consultation and cooperation throughout the area. We are well aware that interdependence is a fact of life throughout most of the world and that it is something that affects us too, whether we always like it or not. And we know that we in the Pacific Islands must continue to act with at least some degree of concert if we are to retain our integrity and avoid being consumed, one by one, by forces much less altruistic than the current regionalist movement. All of this is particularly evident to us as we observe developments in specific areas such as the Law of the Sea, developments that can either assure our economic viability or destroy it.

Hence, we are, in the last analysis, supportive of the regionalist concept so long as it recognizes and accommodates differences between the large and the small, the industrial and the traditional, and maintains sight of the fact that the ultimate end of the process is greater happiness and fulfillment for all the many peoples of the area.

Man does not live by bread alone. The richest and most satisfying experiences are those of the spirit. Let us satisfy basic bodily requirements. Let us provide the facilities for a reasonable life. Let us ensure that there is provision for our children's education. All of these will require planning and money and economic effort by the people themselves. But let us not lose the vision of a Pacific community where people matter, where kinship and other bonds provide an intricate network of benefits and obligations, and where the spirit of man can expand and develop in unique ways.

I leave you with this final thought and thank you for inviting me to express myself on this most important topic.

ASEAN and the Pacific Region

Gerardo P. Sicat

July 30, 1980

Gerardo P. Sicat, minister of economic planning of the Republic of the Philippines, is both a scholar and a government official. His lecture series address illustrates this duality. He opens with a thoughtful review of the historical factors responsible for the region's many differences and disparities. Against this background, he recounts the emergence of the Association of South East Asian Nations (ASEAN) and describes its current status in some detail. He then surveys recent developments within the Pacific regionalist movement and concludes that ASEAN is not yet ready to undertake the leadership role envisioned by so many of the movement's activists. Emphasizing that he is speaking only for himself, he suggests that a regional organization completely separate from ASEAN is in order. Minister Sicat, an economist by training, published a number of works on economic development in the Philippines and Southeast Asia prior to assuming his present position.

I am honored to be part of this series of lectures on the Pacific community organized by the East-West Center. As we are approaching exciting and perhaps dangerous times, I am reminded of the assertion that the future holds the promise of growth and prosperity for the Pacific region countries. It has been said that the coming century will be one of great consequence for the world, and in that century the Pacific nations will play a significant role.

Today the Pacific nations are widely divergent, not only in historical heritage, but also, more important, in their approach to the solution of the problems of the present and future. The major ideologies and religions are contending here. The influences of the

East and West contend and join in this region. This is so whether in the context of Asian and European civilization or in terms of the political and economic forces of the cold war or détente.

The Pacific region is composed of a wide array of countries. To be all inclusive, this area would include the Soviet Union, China, the two Koreas, and Japan on the Northeast Asian rim; Indochina and the archipelagic area that is Southeast Asia, Australia, and New Zealand on the western side of the Pacific. On the eastern shores of the Pacific Ocean are the two Americas, which include the United States, Canada, Mexico, Peru, Chile, and other Latin American countries. There are also island countries and dependencies scattered in the wide expanse of the Pacific Ocean.

Among all these countries, there are different persuasions and orientations; there are different political and economic systems working either in harmony or in potential opposition. Although some countries have contacts with each other—especially with the foremost trading and industrial nations—many of them have not had continuous or substantial economic relations. As a result they are often ignorant about each other. It will take a long time before these countries can have a sense of a Pacific community or of a common destiny.

What common denominators should define a community? And how is that community feeling fostered? Obviously, each country should get to know its neighbors better, and it might begin with cultural and economic contacts.

The ASEAN countries are no exception when it comes to the lack of knowledge of one another. The growth of a feeling of community in ASEAN has begun, but it has taken time to foster this. Only through greater contact within a regional framework has this greater acquaintance grown over time.

ASEAN

The Association of South East Asian Nations came into being after the Bangkok Declaration of August 8, 1967. In that declaration, the five countries that now form the Association—Malaysia, the Philippines, Singapore, and Thailand—decided that a regional organization would bring mutual benefits and stimulate solidarity through regional cooperation. This happened at a time when greater regional cooperation was thought essential. In the words of that declaration, it was desired "to establish a firm foundation for common action to promote regional cooperation." There had been attempts at setting up regional institutions, but the diversity of historical, cultural, religious, and political backgrounds hampered these initial attempts. For despite their regional and geographic affinity, the ASEAN countries are basically the product of different colonial rules, and their institutions and economic patterns reflect these divergent responses to historical influences. Except for Thailand, all the ASEAN countries got their political independence after the Second World War. In fact, for many years the ASEAN neighbors were isolated from each other, being more bound to their respective colonial masters. This led to mutual suspicion, even conflicting designs. Hence, the confrontational atmosphere of the 1960s in the region.

The developments in ASEAN did not obtain full momentum until the mid-seventies. This was the consequence of the preoccupation with other serious regional problems of that time, notably the Vietnam War. However, consultations among the ASEAN partners were held, and on many fronts, but essentially discussions of an economic community, or the need for closer economic cooperation, almost always fell short of inciting decisive action.

Things changed immediately after 1975 with the closing of one chapter of Southeast Asian history, the Vietnam War. Concerned with both the immediate and long-term implications of this historic fact, the ASEAN heads of government decided to hold a summit. The summit meeting in Bali on February 23-24, 1976 provided the political will to support greater economic cooperation. In addition to the meetings of foreign ministers at the political level, which had gone on since ASEAN's birth, the economic ministers of ASEAN were directed by the heads of government to work out agreements relating to regional cooperation affecting food and energy, industrial projects, preferential trading, and joint approaches to international issues. This directive set out the work for the economic ministers on various aspects of economic cooperation and has resulted in a substantial presence of ASEAN in regional issues. Of course the consultation on other issues, especially on political developments in the region, has become closer as a result. In addition to these meetings, the sense of community was extended in meetings of ministers of education, of labor, of social welfare, and of health. A wide array of potential cooperation opened up which was not possible within the framework of bilateral arrangements.

It has been repeatedly observed lately by non-ASEAN observers that the growing cohesion and development of ASEAN is one of the most significant developments in the Pacific region. This is all the more so since ASEAN countries together form a sizable bloc.

In 1977 the combined population of ASEAN was estimated at 240 million in an area of 3,172,000 square kilometers. The per capita incomes of these countries range from $2,880 for Singapore to $300 for Indonesia. The ASEAN countries are mainly middle-income developing countries. There is an immense variety of natural resources (copper, tin, nickel, among others) and primary agricultural commodities (palm oil, coconut oil, natural rubber, agricultural plantations, timber) of significance to world trade originating in ASEAN. Two members of ASEAN, Indonesia and Malaysia, are energy producing and exporting, while recently petroleum resources have been discovered in the Philippines, pointing to an even wider energy base. And Singapore is a petroleum refining base.

The ASEAN countries have shown a remarkable growth in the 1970s at a time when the world economy has suffered setbacks. These countries have attained a growth rate of 6 to 9 percent per year. Their growth derives from the diversity in their economic activity and from the relative restructuring they have undertaken in these difficult times.

The foundations of the economic cohesion they have built through ASEAN will further strengthen these economies. Today they are basically outward looking, and intra-ASEAN trade is still not large. The ASEAN countries trade more with the United States and Japan than among themselves. In 1977 about 52 percent of ASEAN trade was with the U.S. and Japan. Because of the present state of development of the ASEAN members, it will take a long time for intra-ASEAN trade to take on significant proportions and hence to replace the international trade with non-ASEAN countries. But the cooperative endeavors in trade, finance, and industry will likely expand intra-ASEAN trade even as the ASEAN countries continue to trade outside ASEAN.

ASEAN's international trade with the rest of the world is dominated by Japan and the United States. Trade volume with these two countries was stronger in 1977 than in 1972, so it can be deduced that such trade dependence has been increasing. Part of this increase is due to the energy situation, which has caused the U.S. and Japan to increase trade with Indonesia and Malaysia (both oil exporters). But Japan and the United States account for a high proportion of the trade of the other ASEAN countries—the Philippines, 51 percent; Singapore, 40 percent; and Thailand, 38 percent.

ASEAN has gradually strengthened its internal measures of cooperation on a variety of fronts. This cooperation on the economic front is negotiated in five different committees that have been quite active since 1976 under the economic ministers. Among the outstanding achievements so far is the negotiation of an ASEAN Preferential Trading Agreement (PTA), which is currently the framework under which commodity preferential trading is negotiated. To date this has reached 4,325 commodities, and there is interest to expand this preferential list as well as to increase the rate of preferences. Before the end of 1980 more than 10,000 commodities will be covered in the PTA. It will still take a long time to unify tariff rates or to reduce trade barriers completely, but the negotiations have been active.

Another area of great importance is the agreement on industrial complementation. Guidelines have been finished, and the matter of introducing industries, mainly suggested by the private sectors in ASEAN, within this complementation program can proceed. This is different from the agreement to set up large ASEAN industrial projects, which, by their nature, will take time, effort, and perhaps longer negotiations, and which are negotiated in a government-to-government framework.

In addition, agreements of rice reserve stocks have been concluded. All these cooperative ventures have happened while ASEAN was developing greater cohesion on international issues that affect some or all of the members.

With these developments on the intergovernmental front, the private sectors in the ASEAN countries became active. Private institutions, groups, and industries increased their contacts, and lately several ASEAN industry clubs have mushroomed, fostered by the creation of an ASEAN–Chamber of Commerce and Industry, which is ASEAN-wide in membership. These interactions in the private sectors are creating parallel demands upon governmental action to speed up economic cooperation and hence promote a sense of community and economic integration in ASEAN.

As a consequence of this, dialogues are periodically conducted with other significant countries or regional organizations. Recently ASEAN dialogues have taken place with the European Economic Community, Japan, the United States, Australia, Canada, and New Zealand. Aside from achieving their purpose of introducing ASEAN officials to the officials of other countries, these dialogues have further promoted consultations among ASEAN officials.

ASEAN has proven itself to be a viable and active force in the Pacific and Asian region. It has withstood the early problems of heterogeneous backgrounds by seeking common goals and getting members to work closely together. This was achieved slowly, by consensus, and, as it were, like a building being propped up by continuous improvement of the foundation. It has found strength in cooperation through periodic consultations. The extent of this cooperation has been promoted by an increasing attention to the mechanics and form of organization as the need for cooperation became evident in the problems encountered. The internal organization of ASEAN has, as a consequence, strengthened. Yet, at this point in time, it has avoided a large bureaucracy.

ASEAN has a secretariat based in Jakarta and headed by a secretary general. It has an economics bureau in that secretariat. But basically, all the economic cooperation work that ASEAN has achieved so far has been accomplished without the complement of a large bureaucracy. All the economic working committees are housed in different countries, reflecting a division of labor and thereby reducing secretariat expense. Because of the lack of a research and policy staff, all the efforts so far have been based on solidifying the common consensus that could be reached by the negotiating parties.

There is now an on-going feeling that for ASEAN to progress much faster a larger secretariat is needed. But such lack at this time has not deterred the successful negotiation of important agreements which have carried ASEAN so far since 1976.

ASEAN grew slowly but quite steadily. It evolved from regional groupings existing prior to 1967. Today it is still in a transitional phase, and it is likely that as the ASEAN member countries learn to work with each other, the level of economic cooperation on many fronts will expand and intensify. ASEAN operates by consensus and therefore the least common denominator always determines the level of progress. However, it can be said that for the last three years breakthroughs have been achieved, such that the least common denominator in ASEAN has been raised to a level higher than was possible before.

Hence, within ASEAN a strong sense of community has developed. Would ASEAN develop this sense of community further if it now considered its policies within an expanded regional framework? Will the momentum now achieved be stalled? These questions are relevant to ASEAN in viewing other models of the regional action in which it is a part.

It is now essential to turn to the Pacific community idea.

Pacific Community

In recent months, much attention has been paid to the idea of a Pacific community. The *Interim Report of the Pacific Basin Cooperation Study Group* has been circulated. At about the same time that this study group was meeting, the Subcommittee of Asian and Pacific Affairs of the Committee on Foreign Affairs of the U.S. House of Representatives held hearings in which were presented the expert testimonies of Dr. Lawrence Krause of Brookings Institution, Professor Hugh Patrick of Yale University, and President Everett Kleinjans and Dr. Harrison Brown of the East-West Center.

Cooperative work among scholars in the Pacific area has been going on along a wide front. A joint study group of Australia and Japan has been at work on economic relations between Japan, Australia, and the Western Pacific, and a great amount of interaction among economists, academicians, men of affairs, and officials on Pacific trade and development has been going on for at least a decade and a half. My predecessor at this lecture, Professor Kiyoshi Kojima, has been a guiding light in these proposals and discussions since the mid-1960s. Indeed, the late Prime Minister Ohira of Japan and Prime Minister Fraser of Australia specifically referred to cooperation on the Pacific Basin framework in their recent meetings in Manila during the United Nations Conference on Trade and Development, and in Canberra during the late Japanese premier's visit this year.

A common strand in the Pacific community proposals is the growing need for a group or multilateral approach to a number of regional problems. That the economies of the Pacific region have a high degree of interdependence is now established, and this interdependence could be managed more effectively through consultation and cooperation. In view of this, a forum for specific and periodic consultations is suggested. The framework of this consultation is the principal issue at the moment.

There is still ambiguity on the mechanics of achieving this consultation. There is great hesitancy in official circles about making definite proposals, but academic economists and many without governmental responsibilities have resolutely put forward specific proposals. The most specific is that of the Organization for Pacific Trade and Development (OPTAD) sponsored by Peter Drysdale and Hugh Patrick, which would be "a governmental organization with a small administrative apparatus so as not to become heavily bureaucratic, with specific functional Task Forces to handle defined policy-oriented assignments, [and] an informal, consultative, communicative style of operations." This looks like a limited version of the Organization for Economic Cooperation and Development. As to membership, this proposal favors the likeminded, market-economy nations in the region, confined initially to the Asia and Pacific area. (The membership issue seems likely to be a mainspring of debate almost as soon as a Pacific community concept gains credence.) Under the OPTAD model, the socialist countries would be excluded from potential participation, and it is presumed that cooperation would be facilitated by the market orientation of an economy.

There are other components of Pacific community proposals. Some advocates would not favor the organization approach, but would recommend a consultative mechanism on a go-slow pace, perhaps on an ad hoc basis. Others take the view that an evolutionary problem-by-problem approach should be attempted until the problems become broad enough to require group action. But whatever the approach suggested, it seems that there is a strong feeling that the presence of the five ASEAN nations as a group is critical. In fact, it is even suggested obliquely that ASEAN should take a leading role in its formulation. Professor Kojima in his lecture in this series even outlined an ASEAN-Pacific community forum and presented what advantages might develop for ASEAN.

In his view this could lead to a package of aid and capital-enlarging development finance benefiting the ASEAN countries. On the other hand, Lawrence Krause would like to see an intergovernmental institution which is "totally nondiscriminatory in the sense that it would not attempt to bestow economic benefits on participating countries at the expense of nonmember countries outside the region."

The Pacific Basin Cooperation Study Group, chaired by Dr. Saburo Okita before he became foreign minister of Japan, outlined several basic areas of cooperation, but the group initially stayed away from the problem of mechanics of organization, aside from direct hints that the Pacific Basin cooperation organization should be composed of "internationally open countries." The study group proposed that the organization should: (1) promote mutual understanding; (2) promote cooperation in marine development and resource exploitation; (3) promote industrial adjustment; (4) promote economic cooperation and overseas investment; and (5) review monetary problems and improve financial flows. We were made to understand that the Japanese government was studying this, and perhaps the proposal reached a high position on the Japanese agenda while Prime Minister Ohira and Foreign Minister Okita were in office. This is no longer so. However, there is a strong impression left from discussions with Japanese foreign ministry officials that the official attitude is most positive in the promotion of mutual understanding through cultural contacts, even though it prefers either global or bilateral approaches to the rest of the problem areas enumerated, at least in the immediate future.

As for ASEAN, it would seem premature for it to even consider taking an active or leading role in the formation of a Pacific community, whatever its magnitude in membership will be. In the first place, ASEAN has, as its main agenda, the strengthening of its own organization. Second, it wants to pursue its dialogues on a bilateral effort with other groups and countries. These are substantial concerns, and they are taking a great deal of time already. ASEAN has to be convinced that its dialogues are better undertaken within the framework of a wider regional organization and that would take a lot of convincing since its dialogues or consultations are already in progress.

Hence, ASEAN would do better to wait for clear-cut organizational suggestions that emanate from the other Pacific countries. But here the signals from an official level are not specific. There are enough suggestions, but they have been made at a private level. No government—not even Japan—has gone beyond general ideas. And the present suggestions are not enough to offer excitement to ASEAN because they do not go into tangible benefits that ASEAN would wish to consider, except where a framework for discussing regional problems is offered. In the face of these still ambiguous concepts, ASEAN must review its position.

Now, I do not and cannot presume to speak for ASEAN, nor even for my government on this issue. But perhaps I may develop this in the perspective in which it could be perceived by ASEAN. The most important consideration is that this proposal should be palpably beneficial and should demonstrate that from ASEAN's viewpoint the member countries would accomplish more than they do in the present framework. The proposal must, of course, study seriously the possible, the remote, the advantageous as well as the disadvantageous.

It may be offered at this point, before I am accused of gross speculation, that I have dealt on an extensive level in the affairs of ASEAN and to that extent have some idea of the shape of things to come. Where my perception can be wrong is not on the shape, but on the speed, in which things come.

The idea that ASEAN should join only as a group, which is suggested (or assumed) in the proposals made on the Pacific organization, is a recognition of the importance and solidarity of ASEAN. This is an accurate reading. ASEAN has now reached a point in its development where economic developments within the region affecting more than one of the member countries—as any Pacific-wide organization will entail—will be viewed only in the context of ASEAN by the member countries. This is the reason for the active bilateral dialogues that have developed with the principal Pacific countries—the United States, Japan, Australia, New Zealand, and Canada. These periodic dialogues or consultations have of course extended over a wide range of issues, but they invariably include those affecting international trade and access to markets, investments, and development assistance.

Let me call the proposed organization on the Pacific region —whether it is a limited OPTAD involving only Pacific Basin countries, or an organization involving all Pacific nations, including China, the Soviet Union, the two Koreas, and the Latin American countries—let me call it the Pacific organization.

Under present developments, it would seem that this Pacific organization cannot and will not achieve the level of cohesion now existing in ASEAN. Today ASEAN is not a common market in the European Economic Community context, nor a free trade area. It is a preferential trading area extending over a wide range of cooperation—on food, industry, energy, transport, and communications—not only tariff preferences. However, the preferential trading pattern and the periodic consultations among ASEAN members have widened the potential areas of cooperation and have intensified the consultations in which the members are now engaged.

While ASEAN has already reached this stage, it still has to weld the preferential trading patterns more tightly. And today this is a lively issue with ASEAN. The issue cannot be solved by broadening ASEAN with more member countries. From experience, and because of the consensus approach in decision making, five countries are difficult enough, and until they can move forward more fully together, an increase in the number of decision makers will only complicate the ASEAN way to progress.

On the other hand, it is said, or at least officials and economists emphasize, that at least the United States and Japan are pursuing a policy of an open, global, and multilateral international trading system. Hence, they cannot pursue preferential relations. Under this setup, one wonders how special a region the Pacific is, especially if it is only a part (perhaps even a minor part) of the global relations of the Pacific countries.

It is likely, therefore, that the organizational model being proposed can invite the suspicion that it is designed to dilute the issues of bilateral importance to ASEAN without conceding the need of the ASEAN countries for an improvement in the structure of present relationships. For it can be further contended that the ASEAN bilateral dialogues with any Pacific nation are likely to produce better results than a multilateralized consultation system that would include so many parties as to deflect the issues sharply away. For the potential suspicion to disappear, the willingness of the developed Pacific nations to accord a preferential trading pattern—perhaps in the concept of STABEX (a scheme for stabilization of export earnings from principal primary commodities) or of a nonreciprocal preferential trading pattern along the lines of an improved Generalized System of Preferences—may provide a starting point for discussion.

Consultation forums alone cannot yield interesting results or excite participation. During the early 1970s a limited ministerial forum of Southeast Asian countries, together with Japan, held regular consultations on an annual basis. This ministerial consultation reflected the dissatisfaction with the much wider network of countries that the Economic Commission for Asia and the Far East—now the Economic and Social Commission for Asia and the Pacific (ESCAP)—meetings then represented. It became a mini-ESCAP, however, where speech making was invariably the rule of assembly, and the speeches a repetition of the content delivered in the ESCAP general debate. Since agenda were largely consultative and there was little or nothing to negotiate, the meetings did not prove productive. That consultative forum ended after the Vietnam War.

Surely an organization affecting the Pacific must have serious agenda which can lead to negotiations, sooner or later, so that it continues to hold relevant interest for the participants. This will assure that it does not become a stale organization. Another assurance would result if it should reflect a substantial improvement on the consultative forums within and outside the United Nations that are already in existence.

A purely consultative organization stands in contrast with the working principle of ASEAN. At least among the ASEAN committees involved in economic cooperation, there are always important agenda, some quite controversial, others requiring hard thinking because they affect national and regional interests. Meetings have become meaningful because there are no speeches, no hot-air forums, and eventually meetings of ministers are working sessions. Under such a setup, there is a feeling of movement and of progress. This explains why ASEAN has become an exciting organization.

While I have outlined reservations, it is useful to enumerate some features that may make a Pacific organization attractive from an ASEAN viewpoint.

First, the Pacific organization must not attempt to submerge ASEAN's cohesion and identity. In this fashion, ASEAN can continue to improve its own regional organization. This is consistent with, say, any other two or more countries in the Pacific undertaking more intense regional economic cooperation; the same with Korea and Taiwan. The Pacific region organization can exist with many more subregional groupings engaged in preferential or special types of trading arrangement.

Second, a Pacific organization should not serve to nullify the bilateral issues that ASEAN has considered important in its respective dialogues with Pacific countries. It can be suggested that as ASEAN develops its internal identity through the strengthening of intra-ASEAN cooperation, its leverage to raise questions directly with single countries improves immensely. Therefore it would be wary of efforts that diminish such effective leverage. This can be a matter of judgment, but it can be tested only as a forum evolves from a consultative organization.

Third, the Pacific organization should be able to provide a framework for solving common regional problems that cannot be dealt with on a bilateral level. Perhaps this can also mean that the multilateral or regional focus would enhance the solution of bilateral issues that are of interest to ASEAN, but it should initially concentrate on common regional problems. This is not in conflict with the second point concerning the effectiveness of a bilateral approach to problems that ASEAN considers significant. If a problem is broad enough to affect ASEAN and two other countries, such as the exploitation of marine, seabed, and other resources, perhaps a multilateral Pacific forum is better organized to deal with it. Could this hasten some North-South issues within a regional framework that is not feasible in a global context? Perhaps.

I want to close this lecture in the context of global issues that have far-reaching effects on Pacific regional cooperation. My premise is that the long-term political and security interests of developed countries based on the private enterprise system are related to the support that the major Pacific nations have for the development of those countries based on the same economic system. The security network is dependent on sound internal and regional economic development. If this were taken as a correct premise, then the United States, Japan, Australia, Canada, New Zealand, and others of the developed Western world would pay attention to the fundamental issues raised in the "New International Economic Order," by strengthening access to developed-country markets, supporting international and regional development institutions, and increasing development assistance in consonance with the targets of ratio to gross national product that have been reiterated in the recent Brandt Commission Report.

ASEAN definitely looks forward to leadership and influence from the developed Pacific countries, for instance, in strengthening international development institutions, and in increasing the capitalization of the World Bank, the Asian Development Bank, and the common fund. And ASEAN seeks an improvement in the flow of resources and technology from the advanced to the developing countries. Recently there have been glaring shortfalls in the fulfillment of expectations in this area.

I suppose that if only half of the economic resources that were wasted in the Southeast Asian wars of the fifties and the sixties were devoted to improving trade access and development assistance in accordance with a development master plan even much smaller in scale than the Marshall Plan devoted to Europe in the early postwar period, all of Southeast Asia and the Pacific region would be today a far better place to live in. And, perhaps, this would be without the burden of resettling thousands of refugees from the Vietnam-Cambodian war among the developed countries. Indeed, mention of this massive dislocation of humanity is quite a sobering reminder for the conscience of contemporary times. The lessons of history are many. The future costs of a failed war, not to mention the cost in dislocated human lives, is enough of a reminder of the validity of efforts to sustain peaceful cooperation.

Thank you.

Pacific Community: Dream or Reality?
John Grenfell Crawford
September 24, 1980

John Grenfell Crawford, the distinguished Australian economist and educator, served as chairman of the much-noted Pacific Community Seminar which met at Canberra during mid-September 1980. His address in this series, delivered only days after the conclusion of the Canberra gathering, recounts how the session was initiated and organized, explains why it chose to recommend a "hasten slowly" approach to governments of the region, and details the initial organizational steps it proposed, particularly those concerning policy coordination and issues research. Chancellor Crawford, long associated with the Australian National University, and its chancellor since 1976, is the author of numerous works on regional cooperation in the Pacific and is widely recognized as one of the world's leading authorities on the subject.

Tonight I am to speak about dreams and realities relative to the Pacific community, a subject and title I chose prior to my involvement with the recently concluded and much-discussed Pacific Community Seminar at Canberra. I've kept the title, but I freely confess that, because the seminar finished only last week, I will devote the great bulk of the time to giving you some account of it. I will speak principally, but not only, to a summary of conclusions and recommendations prepared by that conference and designed for submission to the governments concerned. These papers are now publicly available, and I've been very happy to provide them to the East-West Center.

I'd like to take the origin of the seminar just a little further than did President Kleinjans in his opening remarks. It rests in the Ohira-Fraser meeting in January in Canberra; but if I explain the actual procedure, then I think the *bona fides* of the venture will be even more understandable to you. I was approached by Dr. Okita of Japan, a friend of long standing and, I understand, of the East-West Center. He was then foreign minister. He asked me, if the prime ministers of Japan and Australia were to request that I mount a seminar at the Australian National University on the Pacific community idea, would I agree to do so. My answer was "Yes, provided the two prime ministers do not attempt to give me instructions about it," and this was accepted.

While there were no instructions, there were some quite acceptable suggestions. One was that it would be appropriate for the seminar to reflect very much the problems of the eleven market economies, including the five countries of the Association of South East Asian Nations (ASEAN), plus the South Pacific. But as to the composition of the seminar—that is, the personnel—I did not receive one instruction. I'd like that kept in mind because it makes the response to the invitations we sent out more interesting and more encouraging. So this was a Japanese initiative in the sense of Dr. Okita's question to which both prime ministers responded very positively. There was one other rider to my acceptance: this was that the Australian government alone provide the sinews of war, namely, the finance. And this was done. So it was a Japanese initiative, accepted by me, taken up by the two prime ministers, and wholly financed by the Australian government.

The organization of the seminar was left to the University. Let me explain the structure because it impressed itself so much on the members that it became part of their recommendations for ongoing activities. We decided to invite three people from each country, treating the South Pacific as one, but with four representatives. The unique feature was the decision to invite the governments concerned to nominate a senior official to participate as a freely speaking member, that is, speaking in his own right. The only obligation that I suggested to the governments was that these people should report back to them their own impressions of the seminar. And they're in the process of doing that now.

I believe this decision to have a government nominee proved to be an important element in the intense interest shown by governments—an interest which we also fostered by personal visits before the seminar. I went to each ASEAN country and called on the available ministers concerned while some of my colleagues went to the others. And, a little amusing perhaps but interesting, the seniority of the officials who attended ranged from deputy prime minister from Thailand, Thanat Khoman, and assistant secretary of state from the United States, Richard Holbrooke, to Dr. Okita, who had, following the death of Mr. Ohira, stepped down from being foreign minister to become, instead, an ambassador extraordinary looking after Japan's foreign and external economic interests. He was nominated by the new government as the senior official from Japan. These three naturally played a significant role, but behaved just as the others, that is, as people expressing their own views but occasionally helping us by explaining the official policies of their governments in recent years.

Now, the only rejection—and I don't want to pretend to you that the world is absolutely perfect—was regrettably by the prime minister of Fiji. But the prime minister of Papua New Guinea eagerly accepted and nominated a quite senior official. The South Pacific Economic Council nominated Dr. E. Gris, its senior official, who is a Papua New Guinean stationed in Fiji. An invited member from Tonga made the third South Pacific representative; a fourth from Western Samoa had to withdraw at the last moment.

So much for the official members. All others [two from each of the countries other than those of the South Pacific] were absolutely the choice of the University. We chose them in the light of known record of interest in the subject. Now, please believe me when I assure you that we chose people known to be skeptical as well as people known to be rather positively inclined towards some future organization. It was not a one-sided selection.

The next important thing to notice is that our invitees also included academics and businessmen. I think the academics slightly outnumbered the others, but the whole mixture of government, academic, and business people in the seminar proved to be a very fruitful one. There was quite an extraordinary degree of ready interchange and frank discussion among the individuals; there was no feeling of government versus the rest. There were a few observers, about half a dozen, principally from the Pacific Basin Economic Council, a private business sector organization, and the Pacific Trade and Development Conference, which comprises mostly academics. But the observers were not participants, so participation was limited to some thirty-six or thirty-seven individuals, and they really took full advantage of the time available. All told, there were five three-hour sessions, lessened only by coffee breaks; but I noticed that the sessions went on during the coffee breaks too. So there was a total of fifteen hours of solid discussion on the basic questions, which we set in advance.

We set the questions for discussion but not the answers. The questions were: First, what is the Pacific community, or, putting it another way, what are the underlying forces that are making people talk about a Pacific community? Why are people talking about this? Second, what are the issues, if any, arising from these forces? Third, which countries are interested, and in what form of organization are they interested? Fourth, and finally, what steps should be taken? The discussion was good. All members without exception took part. There is no record of anyone remaining silent throughout the seminar. I had to bring every session to a close, as the speakers were anxious to continue on.

There were, as I said, four major, long sessions. Acting as the chairman, I opened the fifth session with a review of what seemed to me to be the major conclusions reached in the seminar. Let me say that my statement was vigorously debated, but, even more important, that I was assisted by thoughtful contributions from such people as Dr. Snoh Unakul, formerly of the Reserve Bank in Thailand, who opened the discussion in this session. Before the seminar convened we nominated two people to open each of the four regular sessions, and, to insure there was no thought domination from Canberra, none of these were Australians. They were all visitors.

As I have already said, the discussion was good. I can also tell you the consensus that emerged was very strong, much stronger indeed than any expectation I had before the seminar. Let us discuss this consensus. I'll take the first two questions together. Why are people talking about the Pacific community, and what are the issues? If I review the kind of discussion that took place, I think you'll better understand the nature of the conclusions and, especially, the final decision to recommend proceeding cautiously, although positively.

The group recognized certain things which at first blush appear to negate any sense of community, to really oppose the idea. One is the enormous diversity of language, culture, and history. Another is the great distances that separate some of the Pacific countries, in complete contrast to Europe. Yet another is the very

Pacific Community: Dream or Reality? 67

great differences in economic strength, with two superpowers and a number of developing countries and several, as it were, in the middle. Now, if you just talk about these things, you don't quickly get an explanation of why people are talking about the Pacific community. They give little force to the fact that the Pacific Ocean can be thought of as a unifying factor.

So let's look at the reasons why people are actually talking about some sense of unity in the Pacific. First, however, I'd like to warn against rhetoric on the subject. You know, at least three people have made the statement, "The Pacific community is here. What are we waiting for?" Now, that is in the nature of rhetoric, and I think we can do without that. The fact remains that if it's here, it's here in terms of the economic growth of the area and the economic interdependence of the countries in the Pacific.

The prime motivating force is not a military one, it doesn't directly involve national security. It is, in contrast, a consciousness that the interdependent countries of the Pacific are a major force in the world economy—that the region is characterized by rapid growth—and an awareness of the rise of Japan with its great importance as a market and, on the other hand, its great dependence on the other members of the Pacific. We must not overlook that, because the greatest bargaining weapon the region and its individual countries have with Japan is that Japan is dependent. It has no future without a proper relationship with the rest of the Pacific.

But likewise, and it's not always acknowledged, Japan is a main source of growth for other countries. Even three or four percent growth in Japan provides such a large incentive to the development of other countries, the trading partners, that it assumes great importance for all in the Pacific. But when that growth has been of the order of five or eight percent, then you can see that it is a major factor indeed. While people recognize the United States as a superpower and as the source of some of the problems and issues that I will discuss, there is a developing consciousness of Japan as the upcomer—one or two might even have said "upstart." It is clearly a power that is growing very fast, although still not one that can exist independently of the rest of us. Mention of Japan and the United States should not, incidentally, obscure the growth stories of Taiwan, Hong Kong, and the middle-income industrializing countries including the members of ASEAN. These success stories are a feature of the Pacific that is extremely important. Again, as I'll mention later, the fact that the Pacific contains a ready-made opportunity for North-South dialogue is also a factor of considerable importance as appropriate institutions are developed.

So it's interdependence—the fact that we're all dependent on one another—that is really responsible for most of the talk about a community of interests. It naturally leads to the idea that, because interdependence does have problems and does raise issues, it would be wise to try to solve those issues on the basis of community action. On the one hand, for example, people recognize that the benefits of the growth of Japan have not been spread evenly through the Pacific and might promote—and do promote in some minds—the fear of neocolonialism, or a new "co-prosperity sphere," whether via government or multinationals. On the other hand, there is a clear recognition that the very growth of Japan provides opportunities for increasing the benefits and spreading them more evenly. The issues do lend themselves to substantive cooperation in seeking solutions in which *all* can gain. That thought came through very strongly—through cooperation there need not be losers. Some are inevitably going to gain more than others, but there need not be losers. This was in our minds as we proceeded, step by step, in answering the other questions.

Now, I'm going to read a list of issues that arose in all sessions, but principally in the second. I'm not going to elaborate on any one of them, but there are some eighteen to twenty of them on which there was clear agreement, in some cases that they simply had to be wrestled with, in other instances that they were not so urgent but that the wrestling would offer gains of the kind I talked about. Here's the list from the official record of the seminar:

- Industrialization, trade expansion, structural adjustment, and related questions of protection and trade liberalization
- Energy production, utilization, trade, and research (There was a very heavy request for more help in the areas of energy security, not just for Japan but for a number of countries.)
- Problems of direct investment, including codes of behavior by investors and governments
- Capital markets and financial flows

Pacific Community: Dream or Reality?   69

- Institutional arrangements for Pacific economic cooperation (It was thus early recognized that cooperation calls for some institutional form.)
- Cultural and educational exchange
- The operation of development assistance
- Transport
- Communication
- Food security and related agricultural trade issues
- Mineral security and related trade issues
- Pacific marine resources and how to handle them in the interests of the members of the Pacific Basin
- Scientific and technological exchange
- Relations with China (an issue which was frequently mentioned, not in fear or hostility, but in terms of how best to operate between different types of economies)
- Population movement, including the question of handling of Indo-Chinese refugees
- Matters of special interest to the southwest Pacific Island nations, including questions of transport and communication, their Achilles' heel
- The integrity of ASEAN and the South Pacific Forum in any wider group, a key matter in any institutional development

Now, in discussing these issues it was inevitable that there would be anticipatory discussion of the questions of the later session. It's hard to discuss the issues on this list without talking about what form of institution would best enable the countries concerned to deal with them. There was clear agreement on the need for a set of objectives and "rules of the game"—my own words—applying to the Pacific community. Thus, only halfway through the seminar, these issues not only forced themselves on the minds of the participants, but it was recognized that there had to be some way of cooperating on them. This was, naturally, strongly emphasized in the final two sessions. But before they went on to those other questions, the members recorded some principles, both positive and negative, which really amounted to guiding statements for the remaining sessions. For example, they stressed the need to avoid military security issues because they felt there were no early prospects of area-wide cooperation on this point. They did recognize that a principal objective had to be to foster growth and trade expansion as a way of contributing to the overall peace and prosperity of the region. In this respect the automatic inclusion in the region of countries from both the southern and the northern ends of the so-called North-South relationship was seen as a great advantage. The need to "hasten slowly" emerged strongly as a desirable caution. So, early, before they were actually asked the question, "What organization, what next step?" the hasten slowly principle was clearly expressed by the members. The need to protect existing bilateral, regional, and global mechanisms for cooperation against any undermining was strongly and unanimously accepted.

Two further guidelines, both of particular interest to the East-West Center, were set down. The first concerns the feeling that there should be an organic approach—a building on existing private arrangements already in existence in the Pacific, including such bodies as the Pacific Basin Economic Council, the Pacific Trade and Development Conferences, and also the many institutions such as the East-West Center, the Australian National University, and the institutes in Indonesia and elsewhere that are at present contributing significantly to the solution of the problems of the area. The other guideline, laid down quite early, concerns the very great value seen in ensuring that future dialogue in the Pacific involves what some have called the tripartite arrangement whereby people from government, the universities, and the private sector are included as the best way of insuring that some understanding of the issues and the possible approaches to them will be reached. And, of course, the need to concentrate on regional interests as distinct from purely global questions was stressed. These two guidelines are bound to figure prominently in further intergovernmental exchanges on the Pacific community idea.

Let me turn now to the final two questions. Who would be interested, and in what form of organization? What countries would be interested, and in what form? That was question number three. Now, let me say quite directly and without equivocation, *that* discussion was not a complete discussion, for reasons already indicated. People wanted to proceed cautiously and avoid trying to identify a so-called perfect approach to a permanent organization, as though we have any chance of reaching it very quickly. But two or three things were said, quite unanimously, which make it easier

Pacific Community: Dream or Reality?

to go forward. One was that there was no desire on anyone's part at that seminar for any effort—short or long term—to reproduce the European Economic Community in the Pacific. This concept was nonviable so far as the members of the seminar were concerned, largely on the grounds that it would be pretty-well impossible to achieve that degree of economic unity and, given the inward-looking character of the European Economic Community, there was no real desire to emulate it. The second one was, as it were, a kind of antithesis to that. Having rejected a frequently quoted model, the members wanted to make it clear, nevertheless, that the Pacific nations cannot rest on the proposition of doing nothing. That was one of the questions we put: "Is it better just to do nothing? Let's proceed with bilateralism alone." The answer was a clear negative. We must take some positive steps.

Against this background, the members not unnaturally sidestepped the question of who would be interested in being members of some ultimate body by saying, very sensibly, that the final form of a permanent body would largely determine or influence the membership question. There was some discussion of the Organization for Economic Cooperation and Development and commonwealth models including the Organization for Pacific Trade and Development concept, but none wished to advocate immediate action. Now, that would appear to be avoiding the question of whether China, Russia, the Latin American nations, and so on should be members. That wouldn't be fair. When it came to the actual proposal to set up a standing committee and to have task forces, the principle was laid down immediately that task forces should be open to those people—those nations around the Pacific—with a direct interest in the topic. Regarding marine fisheries, for example, if the Latin American countries, Russia, or China should declare an interest, they could ask to be associated with it. So it was not a negative, exclusive-club attitude; it was a feeling that since we are going cautiously, let us recognize that among the cautious steps there may be scope—there almost certainly will be—for inviting people from countries not represented at this seminar.

So, the final session largely devoted itself to discussing what immediate steps would be productive without prejudicing some ultimate, formal structure for the Pacific community. And here I am turning quite closely to the written text of the recommendations. I won't read it, but I will go through the main points with you. I think I've made it clear that the recommendations are a public document, released by me at the public forum which followed the seminar.

The first point was that since we want a lot of work done, let's strengthen the existing regional and multilateral institutions by supplementing them in the ways necessary to enable them to tackle the regional problems. There was a good deal said about this. In particular, the members wanted quite clearly to establish a habit of cooperation, the specific form of which I'll come to in a minute. They kept saying in their speeches around the table and in their comments, "Please advance step by step, never grandiosely, at every stage. Select priorities as to the issues to be examined, since we cannot tackle them all." Some priorities were identified, and I'll indicate these shortly. As to the mechanism, I want to make it clear that you can call it interim or not as you wish. If you believe there's ultimately going to be a major organization, the steps I'm outlining will be interim only. But a key principle applied by the seminar was that these steps, no matter how long or how briefly they last, should have a value in themselves, should produce worthwhile results regardless of the ultimate outcome of the movement toward a permanent form of intergovernmental organization.

The first recommendation was that a standing committee of about twenty-five persons be established to coordinate an expansion of exchanges of information within the region and to set up task forces to undertake major studies of a number of issues relative to regional cooperation. The seminar suggested that the committee could usefully be called the Pacific Cooperation Committee and it should be unofficial, private, and informal in its proceedings. It would with advantage, the seminar said, have a designated contact institution in each country. The committee should include a mixed group of government, academic, and business persons of considerable authority. Let me reassure anyone who's worried, that there was no thought of the Canberra meeting perpetuating itself. That seminar is over. The composition of any future body is a completely open question, but the seminar did stress the value of a mixed composition for the committee. They did note the fact that having people of considerable authority present was a major help. Dr. Thanat Khoman, Dr. Okita, and Mr. Holbrooke made a

Pacific Community: Dream or Reality?

significant contribution without in any way dominating or monopolizing the various ideas canvassed by the other thirty-three members. It was recognized that the committee, to operate, has to be accepted by governments and has to have secretarial assistance located in some center, maybe where the chairman operates. Decisions have to be made about this. The prime task of the committee was seen as the establishment of task forces reporting back to it and thence to the concerned governments. Now, there is some reflection in this recommendation of both former Secretary Vance's ideas and the Japanese report which came to light just before the seminar, but I think it would have emerged even without these suggestions. Besides setting up its own task forces on the priority issues, it was felt that the committee should also be its own task force, or standing seminar, to carry forward the exploration, discussion, and examination of a more permanent form of intergovernmental cooperation in the Pacific. This was the second major recommendation.

The priority issues nominated for task forces are five in number—trade, investment, energy, marine resources, and international services. Trade includes market access problems and structural adjustment associated with industrialization in the developing countries. I am aware that structural adjustment is a sensitive issue in my own country as indeed it is in the United States and even in Japan. Nevertheless, it does need to be dealt with on the basis of an understanding that the necessary adjustments will not necessarily be confined to the advanced countries. Mutual trade concessions may be possible and should be examined. Hence, it is an issue that requires attention from a task force.

The second issue named was direct investment, for which the only international document of any standing at the moment is a code of behavior drafted by the private sector through the Pacific Basin Economic Council. Now, one doesn't anticipate that that would be completely acceptable to the governments concerned, but let us give them credit for having recognized the need for such a code.

Energy was the third issue nominated. It includes access to markets, assurance of continued and reliable supply, alternative forms, conservation techniques, and research exchanges.

The other two issues nominated for the priority group were Pacific marine resources and international services, the latter referring to air and sea transportation, communication, and education exchanges. I do not have to elaborate on these.

It is significant that the seminar noted, and indeed stressed, the good sense in looking to established research institutions for support in the work of the task forces. It also suggested that an existing institution or group of institutions be strengthened to facilitate an enhanced exchange of information among the various private bodies concerned with regional affairs, including those in the business sector. It also expressed the hope that the Pacific Trade and Development Conference would be able to sustain its activities. An important stimulus for ideas, this body appears to require funds to enable its members to keep in touch between its periodic conferences in various Pacific countries.

Members from the government and private sectors were strong proponents of the need for a next step without committing anyone to a final view about a permanent intergovernmental organization, which, nevertheless, many saw as inevitable at some future time. The important merit of the committee—and I stress it—is the need to start the practice of cooperation. The committee was the seminar's major recommendation and was overwhelmingly supported.

There were many other valuable and interesting views expressed. But the question that has really bothered me throughout —before and since the seminar—is how to get any positive recommendation off the ground. At my insistence, we did briefly discuss the question of how we get this committee off the ground. Now, my obligation as chairman of the seminar, and my obligation to the governments, is to report back to the governments. The immediate report of the actual recommendations has gone. By the time I get back to Australia, I'll consider a draft report of the whole proceedings. But I will be urging the governments of the region to take the recommendations, which are cautious and sensible, quite seriously. I'm glad to say that the Australian foreign minister has already undertaken to pursue the matter and try to ensure, for his part, Pacific-wide consideration of the matter. And I have reason to believe that other governments are already willing to have these matters examined.

The title of my talk was "Pacific Community: Dream or Reality?" Now, Mr. Wolff [formerly of the United States House of Representatives and an advocate of regionalism] is quite right. In a sense it's already a reality, because interdependence has brought us all together whether we like it or not. I think we have realized that we can take advantage of that interdependence and further increase the gains for all of us from trade and investment, better communication, and better educational opportunities. So it's no longer just a dream; but very much has yet to happen before it wholly becomes a reality. I am not pretending, as chairman of the seminar, that we have produced the final thing; but also as chairman of the seminar, I do believe that the seminar—which, I remind you, was comprised of skeptics as well as those in favor of the Pacific community concept—reached a virtually unanimous position that there is a realistic basis on which to go forward. It is a deliberate, cautious position stating that we can begin cooperating together in the solution of real issues. It is the belief that practicing cooperation is the best way to move toward a more permanent structure.

Thank you very much.

Hawaii's Role in the Pacific Community
George R. Ariyoshi
October 22, 1980

George R. Ariyoshi, governor of the state of Hawaii, is another in a long line of public officials from the Islands who have demonstrated an extraordinary concern for international affairs as his address for the lecture series illustrates. Following an impassioned plea for greater attention to the Pacific, he reviews Hawaii's historical role in developing a Pacific consciousness and then ponders the current regional movement. In this context, he questions the staying power of economics as the basic link within the region and wonders if educational cooperation might better serve that purpose. He concludes with the suggestion that the Pacific Cooperation Committee proposed by the recent Pacific Community Seminar in Canberra be located in Hawaii and offers to provide the requisite administrative and technical support. In the light of Hawaii's internationalist record over the years, there can be little doubt that his offer should be seriously considered.

Let me declare emphatically here today that the Age of the Pacific has arrived. It has been a long time—sometimes tragically long—in coming. It has been tragic, because the last three major wars fought by our country were in the Pacific and Asian areas. Certainly global factors were at work, but I have to wonder if a greater understanding of this part of the world might not have altered at least a part of history. Our only recent recognition of the Age of the Pacific is tragic, too, because for far too long our nation has looked to Europe, almost exclusively, for its traditions, for its values, and for its institutions. A majority of the world's population lives in the Pacific-Asian area, and has for centuries. During these centuries, many enlightened cultures have developed. But yet, much of this profound and collected knowledge and thought has been either ignored, belittled, or discarded. Certainly, today there is renewed hope.

This East-West Center, where we are gathered tonight, represents considerable hope and significance. To be sure, the steps taken thus far by the East-West Center in global significance and understanding are the steps of an infant. They are significant in the eyes of the parents, but are not that important to the world overall. But from an infant, an adult grows. A start has been made here. A very significant start. A breakthrough in bureaucracy, in thought, and in attitude has been achieved. A concept has been delineated and defined of what a vast region of the world, containing more people and vastly more geography than any other, can mean to the future of every person born on this planet in the next hundred years. Strong words, but at the same time true words. The efforts and the achievements of the East-West Center, significant as they are, are not the only catalysts at work. Economic, social, geographical, and national events have played a major part in this recognition. But, however it has been achieved, through whatever means, and because of whatever circumstances, our Western world never again will be quite the same because the Age of the Pacific is upon us.

In preparing for this address today, I did some thinking about my personal life and future, as well as that of our region and of our world. I am looking forward with great expectations to my 75th birthday, which admittedly is quite a few years in the future, but which will occur about two decades from now, in the year in which the third millenium and the twenty-first century begin. Thus—if the Good Lord spares me—I will celebrate the diamond jubilee of my own birth in the year 2001.

As I reflect upon this happy coincidence, I am moved to reflect upon what our world will be like in the year 2001. The state of Hawaii established in 1969 a Commission on the Year 2000 which has made, and continues to make, a serious effort to assess Hawaii's future economic, political, cultural, and social systems, to identify desired goals and objectives and the action programs needed to attain those objectives. Our Hawaii State Plan is a prime example of a major, practical, workable outcome of our state's concern for the future—a well-organized preparation for the coming of the twenty-first century. Many organizations, agencies, programs, projects, and individual activities in our Islands continuously work to help Hawaii's people toward a brighter and nobler future. This immense vitality is all around us, constantly interacting, changing, but always thrusting forward with a positive spirit, with a faith and hope that the future will indeed be better as a result of such work.

The Recurring Theme: The Pacific Community

One of the constant signs of this faith and hope for the future is found in the recurring theme, "the Pacific community." In those three words there is expressed a great desire in Hawaii for bringing together peoples in a unity not yet achieved, and to integrate the various structures of our Pacific society by which our peoples interact with each other. This is, indeed, a worthwhile desire.

The genesis of the Pacific community idea goes a considerable way back in Hawaii's history and, I'm sure, in the history of other Pacific regions. But it developed well in Hawaii because of our unique geographical location, and later because of our unique social and ethnic development.

The logic of Hawaii being the heart of the Pacific family of nations and people is now very well known. The specialists in this field can recount the names of one organizational effort after another formed in Hawaii, and elsewhere, in earlier years—the Pacific outreach ideas of Chief Boki and Walter Murray Gibson and King Kalakaua, the Pan-Pacific Union and the Institute of Pacific Relations, Japan's ill-fated Greater East Asia Co-Prosperity Sphere, the many post–World War II organizations, and the more recent rash of Pacific community proposals which have led to the Pacific Basin Economic Council established in 1967, the new Pacific Basin Development Council, and proposals for a Pan-Pacific Community Association and Pacific Cooperation Committee. Recently, numerous other groups have been founded: the Association of South East Asian Nations, the Asian Development Bank, United Nations Economic and Social Commission for Asia and the Pacific, the South Pacific Commission, the South Pacific Forum, and innumerable specialized organizations ranging from the Pacific Area Travel Association to the Pacific Telecommunications Council.

The Yearning for Unity in Freedom

All of these formations and aggregations and groupings attest to the eternal yearning of the human heart for unity, for social interaction, for betterment through cooperative organization. And, significantly enough, it is a yearning expanded and nourished by freedom.

Certainly, we see this in the Pacific Islands, where a number of nations have achieved long-due independence and now wish to harmonize their outreach activities through outreach with others.

It is this new life and new spirit in the Pacific that has brought about renewed interest in the idea of a formalized Pacific community. And this new life and spirit greatly interest Hawaii because of the potential for bringing about greater harmony among Pacific peoples, and for the numerous opportunities offered to Hawaii to contribute significantly to that greater harmony.

A Proliferation of Viewpoints

A recent result of this desire for freedom and unity has been a rash of meetings, conferences, articles, commentaries, and proposals. I'm sure most of you have followed these developments, and I need not recount here the results of the Kuilima conference, the East-West Center conference, the Canberra seminar, or other gatherings or proposals.

What has been going on is intensive talking and intensive soul-searching. And this is good. It is a very human means of getting to the core of complexity, to find out the reality of meanings, intentions, needs, desires, and proposals. This is, indeed, why you are here today: to hear the ideas of the governor of a small state geographically, but the governor of a giant state in terms of human relations, human understanding, and human dignity.

Our region is an integral part of both Polynesia and the United States. This double cultural heritage which is Hawaii's —Polynesian and American (and both aspects are genuine and extensive)—is further enhanced by certain economic and social factors. We are a very progressive, modern state. Hawaii is intellectually, economically, and scientifically sophisticated, and blessed with one of the world's most beautiful physical and climatic environments. While we enjoy these physical blessings, unmatched nearly anywhere, it is our people that are the genius of Hawaii. These islands, to be sure, are a precious jewel set in a great sea of nations and peoples. They are an eminently logical location for Pacific community activities, conferences, and headquarters. Later on I will develop a little more this idea of Hawaii's centrality, suitability, and usefulness in serving an emerging Pacific community structure or organization.

Hindrances to Greater Unity

Right now, however, we must consider certain complex issues which tend to inhibit a greater unity among Pacific peoples and nations. Size and distances are one great issue; the vastness of the Pacific with the practical realities of traveling, meeting, and acting together are serious hindrances to frequent and close consultations. But if we look to the future, telecommunications technology will provide help for us in this regard. Language differences are another difficulty, but again, the technology of the future should be able to change our present Tower of Babel into a hall of greater linguistic uniformity. Still another problem is the question of who speaks for one's nation and one's people. Democracies have their legislatures and executive and judicial branches, and these systems—believed to be the best yet devised for the freedom of peoples—are cumbersome for getting things done efficiently.

Assuming these problems can be overcome—and they are primarily technical problems—we still face deeper difficulties. In any Pacific community organization, who shall merit membership and by what mechanism will membership be granted or withheld? What degree of power or influence will be wielded, and what authority will exercise such power? And what philosophy —among many philosophies and cultural traditions—shall dominate?

It is one thing to propose, for instance, that we unite Japan, Korea, Peru, Western Samoa, New Zealand, and Papua New Guinea in a union of trade, commerce, and mutual understanding. It's very much another thing to accept the actual dynamics and purpose of Japanese trade or Korean commercial expansion in the small communities of Micronesia or in the volatile political climates of South American countries.

Economic Links Can Help But . . .

So far, a great common denominator which tends to unify our patch-quilt Pacific world is money, profit, and entrepreneurship. This should not be looked upon as intrinsically wrong. It should, however, be seen not as an end in itself, but as a means toward a much greater purpose, that of social harmony and the true advancement of peoples.

Too often trade operates in a vacuum without a clearly expressed philosophy or acceptable social purpose. The Soviet Union has its own reasons for trade and commerce; the United States may have others. In American Samoa, for instance, where most of the land is communally owned, private property and profit are viewed differently from the way they are viewed in California. And there are mixed opinions about motivations behind promoting trade in countries with multinational corporations.

The point I wish to make is this: in considering the formalization of a Pacific community, perhaps we should look not so much for the means to carry out preconceived notions of what is good and valuable for communities of peoples, such as increased trade, but rather search first for principles upon which unity and harmony can be structured and make it perhaps a lifetime of work to educate all to the meaning and value of such principles. I suggest that in the long process of doing this, the trade and commerce will logically follow—and in very good measure.

The United Nations has sought to do this, and its charter reflects the wisdom of its founders in delineating a fundamental philosophy and beautiful purposes. These include the maintenance of peace and security among nations, the development of friendly relations between nations based on the principles of equal rights and self-determination of peoples. The U.N., it seems to me, is above all a primary global educational institution which achieves its peak of greatness when it educates people to understand the tremendous dimensions of their nobility and potential.

Education: The Primary Thrust

In proposing this idea that there be primary emphasis on the educative process, I recall the words of the late Governor John A. Burns. He referred to a "subtle inferiority of spirit" among many in Hawaii. He meant this to be, I'm sure, a gentle rebuke to our fellow citizens who do not realize, or understand, their potential for leadership in a world which sorely needs good leadership. I believe Governor Burns might have felt the same way about other island peoples in the Pacific whose basic integrity, wisdom, prudence, compassion, and other leadership qualities, if developed, could transform our Pacific world.

There is an enormous and enduring need for educating millions to understand their potential, so they may exercise in freedom their special talents and abilities to improve our world through intelligent interaction with others. And therefore, I submit that the primary thrust of any Pacific community cooperation and organization work be educative.

We must never forget two things: we live in the computer age, and the world's greatest computers rest on the shoulders of millions of people who only need their computers linked and integrated to perform great new economic and social wonders.

Hawaii's experience in, and facilities for, education are already superb and ideally suited to such a Pacific task. In the Islands, public and private educational resources have given our own people both splendid educational opportunities, and a deeper appreciation of education's multiple benefits. These opportunities range from the only completely state-run and statewide public school system in the United States, to a very fine system of parochial and private schools, to public and private university facilities, including dynamic community colleges, and on up to our East-West Center.

Hawaii: The Ideal Location

This leads me back to what I mentioned earlier in my address: Hawaii's centrality, suitability, and usefulness in serving an emerging Pacific community structure or organization.

Hawaii's many attributes are, indeed, extraordinary for such a task. Our geography and climate are ideal for serving as a center for Pacific regional activities. We are distant enough from other land masses that our waters and air are among the purest on the globe, and yet modern transportation and communication put us in almost instant touch with any part of the globe.

Hawaii has developed the practical, sophisticated hardware and infrastructure for travel and communication by literally millions of people. Each year a large percentage of our own people confidently leave the Islands routinely for business or vacations. This year and last year combined, close to eight million people will have visited our Islands. They were transported, fed, housed, entertained, and sent home again with the warmest of memories of their Island visit. They came from east and west, north and south, and what they found here—nearly all of them—was much more than greenery and scenery.

Hawaii's Greatest Asset

Our visitors found in Hawaii a community of people wise in the ways of the world—with that special wisdom which is found only among a people whose familial roots lie in distant lands and cultures.

Hawaii is Polynesian-American, but it is also Micronesian- and Melanesian-American, European-American, North-, Central-, and South-American, Australian- and New Zealand-American, and many others. Hawaii's peoples are at home with peoples of other lands, and their composition stems from the people of other lands. Thus, for many reasons, Hawaii is a most logical place for the headquarters of Pacific community organizations.

I invite all of you to write to me to express your thoughts on the formation of a Pacific community advisory committee which could explore the various questions relating to this subject. I have in mind an ad hoc think tank which will not be limited by the constraints of a time frame or deadline, yet will be a group which keeps up to date on the many ramifications of the developing idea of a Pacific community and will provide the broadest possible insights to all who will at various times need such information and wisdom.

We must keep in mind that there may be a bit of a letdown in interest following the recent intensive activities concerning Pacific interaction and cooperation.

There remains the compelling idea that greater cooperation and unity are necessary, good, and possible, but implementation remains a great puzzle. For example, in recent Pacific community discussions, people have asked whether the Soviet Union and China should be members; whether Japan and the United States would overwhelmingly dominate any grouping of nations, especially small independent island nations of the Pacific; and how shall small nations with a keen sense of their own dignity and worth demonstrate to powerful industrial nations the superiority of their relatively quiet way of life.

I have a personal conviction that Hawaii should be the permanent site for a Pacific community secretariat. More and more we read of the need for such a structure. The most recent activity in this regard was the excellent Pacific Community Seminar sponsored by the Australian government, September 15 through 17 this year, in Canberra. Participants from the United States, Canada, Japan, Indonesia, Singapore, Australia, New Zealand, Thailand, Malaysia, the Philippines, Pacific Island nations, and the Republic of Korea were joined by various observers from regional institutions, all meeting under the auspices of the Australian government. Following its intensive discussions, it recommended establishment of a Pacific Cooperation Committee. The committee would need secretarial assistance as it undertook to expand information exchanges among members and to set up task forces to undertake essential studies leading to increased regional cooperation.

Hawaii would, indeed, welcome the opportunity to serve such a prestigious committee, not only in the administrative or technical sense, but in the broader aspect of becoming its home here in the heart of the Pacific family of nations. I have already given you the logic of Hawaii's serving in this role, and Hawaii's preeminent qualifications.

Let me close by saying how grateful I am to all who seek greater Pacific unity and cooperation. It is a mark of our troubled times that such optimism for the future seems to become stronger as life's challenges become more frequent. As for myself, I offered enthusiasm for my own future. I'm looking forward to the year 2001, not merely to the diamond jubilee of my birth, but to the reality of a greatly improved Pacific region.

Mahalo and aloha.

Prospects for a Pacific Community
Michael Mansfield
February 19, 1981

Michael "Mike" Mansfield, long the majority leader in the United States Senate and presently ambassador to Japan, is widely regarded as an astute and informed observer of international affairs in the Pacific Basin. His address suggests why. The principal factors responsible for the development of the Pacific community movement as well as its current status are quickly and sharply sketched. Major impediments to a more rapid course of action are discussed in some detail as background to a concluding warning that any effort to unduly speed progress could threaten the entire process. While some will find his caution disappointing, it must be given extensive and careful consideration. Few persons anywhere are in a better position to assess the movement in relation to its broader political context and, hence, provide counsel with respect to a viable course of action.

It is an honor and a pleasure to be speaking to you tonight as one of the participants in the East-West Center's Pacific Community Lecture Series. Since its establishment in 1960, the Center for Cultural and Technical Interchange between East and West has worked to promote better relations and understanding among the peoples of Asia, the Pacific, and the United States through cooperative study, training, and research. Those persons who take part in the Center's activities come from over forty countries from the Asian continent and the Pacific. Financial support for the Center is provided by twenty-two nations. The East-West Center is truly an international enterprise guided by a spirit of cooperation among peoples of countries separated by great geographic distances and cultural differences.

It can be said that it is that spirit of cooperation which has inspired and kept alive the concept of a Pacific Basin community. Most of you are at least as familiar as I am with the history of the interest in an institution to encompass the nations of the Pacific Basin in an economic grouping to promote the common good. I want to take a few moments to talk about some of its main points.

The concept of a community is the result of economic reality. The level of economic interdependence among the nations of Asia and the Pacific is high:

- Most of the nations of the Pacific depend on regional markets for more than 50 percent of their exports.
- Indonesia's Pacific markets account for 80 percent of its exports, and for Singapore, the Philippines, South Korea, and Taiwan, the figure is over 70 percent.

Moreover, the development strategies of many of the East and Southeast Asian countries concentrate on trade, and Japan's share of regional trade has been growing consistently. Recent developments in Japan's commercial relations with Mexico may well lead to greater involvement by that Pacific nation in the East Asian economy.

The United States is also a Pacific nation. We have, however, long directed our attention toward Europe. But beginning in the 1970s, American trade across the Pacific surpassed trade with Europe; Japan is now the United States' largest overseas trading partner, while five other Asian and Pacific nations are in the top twenty. American investment in East Asia has been growing consistently, and the returns on the investments have been more profitable than the world-wide average. U.S. trade with the European Common Market nations totaled $89.7 billion in 1980, but the figure for East Asian trade was $113.9 billion. Over the years 1976-1979, the aggregate rate of return for U.S. investments in East Asia was 19.1 percent. This can be compared with 17.1 percent in Japan and 16.3 percent for investments outside East Asia. With such a level of economic activity, interest in establishing an institutional framework to promote and regulate it for the common advantage was only natural.

I would like to look at what is the most detailed official proposal for a community to date. The late prime minister of Japan,

Masayoshi Ohira, in 1978 proposed a "Pacific community" including Japan, the United States, Canada, Australia, New Zealand, the ASEAN nations and other East Asian countries. The purpose of the community would be to promote the region's economic growth. This proposal led to the establishment of a mixed government and private commission, headed by Mr. Saburo Okita, to study the concept and its implications. In its report, released in May of 1980, the Commission observes that "Remarkable progress in communication and transport technologies has turned the vast Pacific Ocean into an inland sea and ordered conditions so that the Pacific countries can create a regional community." The report maintains that the Japanese concept of a Pacific community does not close the region off from other international arrangements, but is rather a means to integrate the region more closely with the rest of the world. It also states that a Pacific community would be an excellent forum for working on the North-South relationship. It would also complement the bilateral and multilateral relations already in existence in the area.

Positing such a Pacific community, the Commission goes on to describe several tasks for Pacific Basin cooperation. Some are "to be dealt with jointly by the countries concerned, while on others Japan should take the initiative for its own action." These tasks include:

- various cultural exchange programs;
- the "internationalization" of Japanese universities;
- the establishment of a "Technical Cooperation Center" to facilitate transfer of technology and human resources; and
- creation of various institutions to promote regional cooperation in the development of natural resources.

Reflecting the constantly growing economic activity in the area, the Commission's report recommends the drafting of a "Pacific Declaration on Trade and International Investment." The purpose of the declaration is to promote trade and encourage positive adjustment of the industrial structures of the nations involved. A "Pacific Industrial Policy Consultative Forum" would be created to discuss the actual implementation of the declaration.

Other tasks in the economic and financial field envisioned for a Pacific community include:

- the establishment of international financial markets in the East Asian area;
- the amelioration of the investment climate in the region; and
- increasing official development assistance to the developing nations.

As regards the concrete measures to be taken in order to accomplish these tasks, the Commission observes that "Pacific Basin cooperation should not be promoted hastily, but carefully and steadily through the gradual congealing of broad international consensus." It recommends the establishment of a nongovernmental committee of fifteen to twenty experts from the nations involved, to serve as the steering body for subsequent international conferences on the Pacific Basin community concept.

The Commission expresses the hope that this steering committee might become a permanent organization, expressing joint opinions or making recommendations to the governments involved on matters relating to Pacific Basin cooperation. Alongside this committee, working groups of specialists would be formed, at governmental or private levels, to promote cooperative projects in areas of specific concern.

The Commission's report concludes with these words: "The next step might be to examine the possibility of establishing an international organization for Pacific Basin cooperation among the governments of the countries concerned."

Japan has taken the lead in presenting a unified official view on the Pacific Basin community. It has recommended substantial governmental involvement in a possible international organization encompassing the Pacific nations. I think the proposal by the Japanese Commission is based on an accurate assessment of the economic and political situation in the Pacific Basin. I especially want to commend its commitment to increase assistance to the developing countries.

Interest in a Pacific Basin community has certainly not been lacking in the United States. It is true, however, that this interest has been concentrated in groups or individuals with a great degree of involvement in the Pacific region. At the same time, the focus of this interest is varied. It has also tended to reflect the particular in-

Prospects for a Pacific Community

terests and fields of competence of the persons or institutions who have promoted the concept.

The reasons for American interest in the concept are, of course, many. Some of these are:

- the growing importance of East Asia and the Pacific nations as trading partners of the United States;
- the population shift to the "Sun Belt," including states of the Pacific littoral;
- dissatisfaction with previous American policy toward Asian and Pacific nations; and
- finally, a profound change in the political climate in the Pacific, which made American participation in a Pacific community both desirable and feasible.

This change certainly includes the establishment of full diplomatic relations between the U.S. and the People's Republic of China. This removed the fear that any American interest in an organization for Pacific cooperation would only evoke a harshly critical reaction from the PRC. At the same time, clear evidence of the desire by ASEAN and other East Asian nations for a higher American profile in the region has provided added impetus to American interest in participation in a Pacific Basin community.

The creation of such organizations as the private-sector Pacific Basin Economic Council (PBEC) and the Pacific Trade and Development Conference kept the interest in the concept very much alive. One of the most active groups in this context has been the U.S. National Committee of the PBEC. It has been promoting broader public understanding of the Pacific Basin economic issues and greater governmental attention to the potential of Pacific cooperation.

As tonight's forum shows, the academic community has been at the forefront of promoting consideration of the Pacific Basin community in the United States. The East-West Center has been one of the central points for activities related to the concept in this country. The Center's work can be used as a model for a gradual approach to the establishment of a community, building on workshops, conferences, and meetings of small groups of specialists.

William Watts has written that the first step in forming a Pacific Basin community is to correct what he considers a grave level of ignorance about East Asia among Americans. He suggests creating a nongovernmental "Council of the Pacific," with participation by national groups composed of individuals from business, labor, academia, and government, to exchange information and ideas on Pacific Basin cooperation.

In several studies promoted in part by congressional interest, particularly that of Senators Glenn and Roth and former Representative Wolff, American specialists with a common interest in Pacific and East Asian affairs have made suggestions for the institutionalization of a Pacific Basin community. Ambassador Richard Sneider has recommended the establishment of an intergovernmental consultative institution, organized loosely along the lines of ASEAN, which would concentrate on economic issues. In separate papers presented to Congress, Lawrence Krause, Hugh Patrick, and Peter Drysdale introduced to the United States the idea, which originated in Japan and Australia, of an Organization for Pacific Trade and Development (OPTAD), resembling the Organization for Economic Cooperation and Development in structure. OPTAD is seen as an intergovernmental consultative forum with a small secretariat and task forces for specific economic issues.

This has been a rather superficial overview of the idea of the Pacific Basin community concept in Japan and the United States. I have spoken of these two countries because for a long time it has been the industrialized nations that have been promoting the concept of Pacific cooperation.

This is no longer the case. The developing nations have begun to make their voices heard ever more loudly in international forums where the matter has been discussed. The ASEAN nations have generated many productive ideas about a Pacific Basin community. From the very beginning, the ASEAN nations have been seen as indispensable members of any such arrangement, because of their outstanding economic potential, rapid growth, and their successful regional association. ASEAN is a purely voluntary association which fully respects each member country's sovereignty and existing bilateral agreements, and which exists exclusively for the promotion of the common interests of the member nations.

ASEAN spokesmen, both from the government and private sectors, have voiced various cautions about an institutionalized

Prospects for a Pacific Community

Pacific Basin community. In the first place, there is the concern that any new international organization might overshadow ASEAN and weaken it, depriving it of the opportunity to attain its full potential as an international body.

Also, some ASEAN spokesmen fear that a Pacific community organization might be used to maintain the differences in wealth between the developed countries of the Pacific Basin and ASEAN, keeping the latter in a dependent relationship. On the other hand, ASEAN's Pacific community supporters do not want it to be only a consultative forum, but an organization with full governmental participation and commitments. The developing nations might employ such an organization to promote accelerated transfer of technology and knowledge.

Of course, overcoming these concerns of the developing nations is not the only obstacle facing the proponents of a Pacific Basin community. The most obvious obstacle is the scope of the community. Despite the assertion of the Japanese Commission's report, it is a little premature to call the Pacific Ocean an "inland sea." The Pacific Basin is immense geographically, and its nations are tremendously diverse in terms of language, culture, political institutions, and economic arrangements. While most proposals for a community have centered on the United States, Canada, Japan, Australia, New Zealand, ASEAN, and South Korea, we cannot overlook the fact that very many Asian and Pacific nations are left out of that accounting, or that four South American nations, six Central American countries, and another North American giant, Mexico, form part of the Pacific Basin. The many island groups of the Pacific which are now making their transition to independence also deserve full consideration in any model of an institutionalized Pacific Basin community.

There is also concern that the community would become too narrowly regional, distracting the nations involved from the realities and obligations of global interdependence.

The question of the scope of the community is probably central to the chances of the community's becoming a reality. Since the community has been seen almost universally as an economic grouping, the question of economic orientation of prospective member nations is a fundamental concern. Specifically, what would the community's position be on the inclusion of centrally directed economies, and in what way would the centrally directed economies interact with the market economies in the community? Any Pacific Basin economic grouping which does not make some provision for dealing with the centrally directed economies would run the risk of being perceived by those nations as more political than economic.

Such a danger must be given serious consideration, especially when we look at the present political situation in Asia. Vietnam appears to be in control of all of Indochina, a condition which China as well as ASEAN perceives as destabilizing. The PRC, which has made its opposition to Vietnam's policies quite clear, is experiencing continued tensions with the Soviet Union. The Soviet Union's continued military presence in Afghanistan threatens the stability not only of the Asian mainland but also of Europe. Under such political conditions, the success of an intergovernmental Pacific Basin community is uncertain now.

Leaving aside the question of whether the United States supports any specific design for a Pacific community, there can be no doubt that we support an international atmosphere in Asia and the Pacific that would be a prerequisite for the success of the community. Such an atmosphere would require stability both internally and regionally, a trend of continued economic development, and a recognition of growing interdependence. The indispensable foundations for economic cooperation and growth are peace and stability, and the United States is dedicated to those fundamentals.

As we work to achieve the goals of stability and economic growth, we can see that the present situation in the economies of the Pacific Basin—continued growth, a high level of regional trade and investment, and great awareness of interdependence—has established an appreciation of common interests and concerns, and a framework of governmental and nongovernmental arrangements to deal with these issues. In fact, many observers claim that a Pacific Basin community already exists.

I believe that it would be too hasty to move now for a Pacific community organization on the governmental level. The community, by its very nature, cannot be promoted only by one or two countries. If it is to be successful a great number of its likely member nations must perceive that it is needed. Proponents of the community concept have to involve as many prospective members as possible in the elaboration of the idea. Private organizations, such as the PBEC and the East-West Center, have done the greatest amount of work in defining the objectives and possible structures of an institutionalized community. They are the best venues for the continued discussion and elaboration of designs of the community. Nongovernmental activity is less likely to arouse fears of diminished sovereignty which several nations have voiced. It is also free to consider a wider range of possibilities.

In the meantime, it is up to us who are in the service of our governments to pursue and promote policies which will lead to greater international stability and increased prosperity for the nations of the Pacific Basin.

Thank you.

The Pacific Islands in a Latin American Perspective: Towards a Special Relationship?
Francisco Orrego Vicuña

Francisco Orrego Vicuña, director of the Institute of International Studies at the University of Chile, is among Latin America's best-known authorities on the Pacific Basin. His paper, originally published in 1979 in the first volume of *La Comunidad Del Pacifico En Perspectiva* and reprinted here with minor stylistic changes by permission of the author, opens with a summary of the key points of friction in the relationship between the Pacific Island nations and the major powers with interests in the region. It suggests that a new relationship with the Pacific slope nations of Latin America might thus be of interest to the island states. Preferential trade relations, intermediate technology transfer, communications development, and consultation on maritime, mineral, and political matters are discussed as possible areas of cooperation. The paper also makes a strong plea for a greater consideration of Latin America in all deliberations concerning the Pacific.

Nationalism and Regional Identification in the Pacific Islands

In the immensity of the Pacific Ocean a new community of nations has lately begun to emerge. Today the Pacific Islands are showing signs of a rebirth of their own identity and a growing spirit of solidarity, on which this nascent community is based.

Unquestionably, it is from many points of view a heterogeneous grouping. Geographically it extends over the length and breadth of a vast expanse of ocean, which some writers have identified as "Tropical Oceania."[1] In terms of races, languages, and cultures, too, the diversity is great. Politically, emancipation from colonialism and other phenomena have given rise to many different types of territorial status, ranging from that of independent states to that of trust territories, and including such varied forms as condominium, self-government, and overseas territory.

The elements of identity, however, would seem to be gaining greater strength than those of heterogeneity. To start with, geographical distances are being rapidly bridged by the development of communications, which would be yet further augmented by the establishment of shipping lines and the expansion of air transport services in the Pacific Basin. Progress towards independence will make this status, with few exceptions, a common denominator in the very near future. Even in the cultural field, vast areas of the Pacific Islands share common traditions.

Still more important is the fact that observable throughout the Pacific Islands is the burgeoning of a nationalist sentiment proper to a postemancipation period. This will cause a few difficulties of a secessionist character,[2] although they would not appear to be of major significance. But at the same time it imbues the region as a whole with a sense of identity that the long years of colonial domination had somewhat impeded. The nationalism of the Pacific Islands will be one of the factors that help to strengthen the ties linking up this community in the years to come.

Perhaps for this very reason, the Pacific Island nations do not seem overanxious to identify themselves with the great continental land masses that lie relatively close at hand. Thus, while a considerable proportion of the Pacific Islands is situated in the neighborhood of Asia, it has nevertheless succeeded in maintaining its individuality and cannot be assimilated with the continent in question, though to some extent sharing with it common institutions. This is still truer of the United States, with the exceptions deriving from state linkups and other modes of association. Australia and New Zealand constitute a special case, which will be discussed later, like the potential case of Latin America. Thus, the Pacific Islands are essentially identified with their own geographical ambit. Notwithstanding any associations for which there may be a place, this reality also exerts a decisive influence on the development of the concept of community.

A case in point is afforded by Papua New Guinea, a country which on account of its geographical location might have opted for identification with Asia or with Australia. Nevertheless, even prior to its independence it laid emphasis on the concept of the "priority of the Pacific," as its minister for foreign affairs, Sir Maori Kiki, declared in 1974 in the following terms: "Our first priority has been to identify Papua New Guinea clearly with the island nations of the Pacific who meet regularly in the South Pacific Forum. We feel that these nations are our closest ethnic neighbors and that Papua New Guinea's interests are best served in international affairs by our being clearly a member of the community of the South Pacific island nations, loyal to this community's causes and common initiatives. Such a position, in our Government's view, needs no special defense."[3]

Moreover, the hard facts of economics have also created problems common to these nations, and this is yet another factor that draws them together. The Honorable Tupuola Efi, prime minister of Western Samoa, defined the common problems and characteristics of the Pacific Island nations as follows: "For the island nations of the South Pacific there are some common characteristics: (a) smallness in area and population; (b) limited land-based resources; (c) remoteness and isolation both from each other and from the rest of the world; (d) proneness to natural disasters; (e) small domestic markets and reliance on a relatively small population; (f) extreme dependence on external trade; (g) balance-of-payments problems."[4]

It is interesting to note that while this is typically a developing region, as is shown by the characteristics listed, it is virtually surrounded by industrialized nations and lacks any direct geographical linkage with other developing areas. The presence of the United States, the Soviet Union, Japan, China, Australia, and New Zealand bears eloquent witness to this effect. The countries that are members of the Association of South East Asian Nations (ASEAN) have up to now kept within a mainly Asiatic sphere without establishing a relation of any real importance with other regions. This situation, besides affecting international cooperation programs and the region's international economic and political relations, is of very special significance for the Latin American nations with Pacific coastlines, such as Chile. Despite their geographical remoteness, they represent a potential alternative in terms of linkage of the Pacific Islands with other developing areas; an alternative which, as will be shown, does not represent a substitute for other relationships, but does open up the possibility of a meaningful complementarity.

The Changing Role of the Traditional Powers

To understand the potential role of a relationship between the Pacific Islands and Latin America, reference must first be made to the international framework in which the community in question is evolving, and specifically to its relations with the powers operating in the area.

The first important case that must be mentioned is that of the United States, both because of the vast geographical expanse over which its presence extends and because of the strategic and economic preponderance it assumed during and after the Second World War.[5] Its role in the region has been rapidly dwindling in recent years, partly on account of the decolonization process and partly because the United States administration is losing interest. Micronesia, hitherto a trust territory of the United States, is moving towards independence, or at least towards self-government,[6] in a framework of difficult negotiations which have not always been particularly clean. Thus, the presence of the United States is essentially concentrated in the Marianas group, which is steering towards association with the U.S. as a commonwealth; in Guam, which is the territory that has the closest ties with the United States; and in American Samoa.

Up to now the United States' interest in the region has been prompted by essentially strategic motives, but in relation to its Asian policy, not to the region itself. That is, the Pacific Islands carried weight in Washington's policy insofar as they could justifiably play their role as a bridge for the pursuit of United States policy towards Asia. As the United States began its strategic withdrawal from Asia, its strategic interest in the Pacific Islands itself diminished, except with regard to Guam and other very specific geographical points. This strategic instrumentalization of the Pacific Islands has been repeated by other powers too, as will be seen. The result has been, moreover, that the United States' economic support for the region is no longer a significant factor in the relationship existing today, save for mainly occasional exceptions.

Recently, however, a new factor of special interest has come to the fore in the area: its influence in terms of maritime jurisdiction.[7] In view of the enormous geographical extent of the region, with the application of a 200-mile exclusive economic zone and archipelagic delimitation criteria, an immensity of ocean space comes under national jurisdiction, with all its significance in terms of fisheries and of potential development of mineral resources of the seabed. It is hardly likely, however, that the United States will now be able to exploit this new dimension of the Pacific Islands, despite its interest in doing so, since the blunders committed in its fishing policy have created acute tension between it and the whole of the Pacific Islands, including the independent nations, just as happened some years ago in the case of Latin America, which will be considered later.

Hence it appears that the Pacific Islands can no longer look especially to the United States as the basis for a relationship which will enable them to attain their development and cooperation objectives. Undoubtedly, the presence of the United States in the area will always be important, but it will not represent a special priority, differing from the relations that this country maintains with other developing regions. In the words of an Australian writer, "for the foreseeable future, on present indications the implications of the Carter administration for the Pacific Islands are for a continuation of the disinterest of the past quarter-century."[8]

The Soviet Union has not exercised any special influence in the Pacific Islands area.[9] From the angle of strategy, hitherto the area has fulfilled no function of interest for the USSR in relation to its policy towards Asia, a continent where its presence is direct. But the development of its naval strategy and presence might bring about changes in the region's function in the future. The field in which the Soviet Union does display definite interest is that of utilization of the resources of the sea, with particular reference to fishing and the operation of its fishing fleet. In 1976 it began negotiating an agreement with Tonga for the granting of facilities to its fishing fleet, which provoked a sharp reaction on the part of New Zealand and Australia, but not from the United States, to whom the problem was posed in the framework of ANZUS.[10] The future trend would seem to be towards an increase in the Soviet Union's interest in the area, particularly if it succeeds in consolidating its presence in Southeast Asia.

The People's Republic of China has not been especially present in the Pacific Islands either, but here again it is possible that the position may change commensurately with the development and internal consolidation of China and particularly the strategic stabilization of Asia.[11] At the same time, China's increasing economic and political links with the outside world will probably exert an influence in this direction. Important steps have already been taken in relation to ASEAN, Australia, New Zealand, and Latin America, in addition, of course, to Japan and the United States; it would not appear unlikely that the Pacific Islands too may join this cooperation network in the future.

Another protagonist in the Pacific Islands area is Japan.[12] Since the experience of the Second World War, Japan has been particularly careful to avoid any political manifestation in its foreign relations in general, an attitude which has probably been especially necessary in this area, which was considerably affected by the experience in question. Thus, the content of relations with Japan has been principally of an economic nature. But even on this level relations have not been easy, any more than they have been with other developing countries, owing to the tendency of Japanese entrepreneurs to penetrate too far into the local economies, often without taking into account the needs of the country concerned, and not infrequently causing serious deterioration of the environment.

This policy has begun to undergo modification in recent years, particularly as a result of the difficulties that have arisen in the countries of ASEAN, so that there are grounds for hoping that in the Pacific Islands likewise it will no longer be a source of friction and conflict. One of the areas in which Japan too has shown particular interest is that of fishing and utilization of ocean resources, and this once again confers on the Pacific Island countries an important international role.[13] Here again, however, the handling of affairs has given rise to difficulties with several countries of the region, in connection, for instance, with aviation.[14]

Despite the essentially economic character of these relations, in some official Japanese theses a marked tendency to identify the Pacific with Asia is observable,[15] and might be indicative of interest in the establishment of an area of influence in the region. If it were so, such a policy would probably have to be to some extent concerted with Australia, a country which plays an active role in the area.[16] In any event, the Pacific Islands would in no way benefit by the establishment of two poles of influence of this kind, which, moreover, would probably clash with the nationalist sentiment and sense of regional identification to which reference has already been made.

The role of the traditional powers—the United Kingdom and France—has also undergone rapid change in the Pacific Islands area. The presence of the United Kingdom is nowadays greatly restricted since, in consequence of the decolonizing process and the British military withdrawal east of Suez, the territories retained by the United Kingdom are small in size and few in number. This is offset, however, by the existence of strong links at the level of the Commonwealth, of which many of the countries of the region are members,[17] and by economic activity, in which again the United Kingdom has steadily maintained its participation. Another aspect that must not be forgotten is the economic and commercial role enacted in this field by the European Economic Community, with which many of the countries of the region are linked through trade association mechanisms.

France makes its presence more intensely felt,[18] especially in the territories of French Polynesia and New Caledonia (the major nickel producer). The New Hebrides, a French-British condominium, are approaching independence.[19] Although the role of France in the Pacific was seriously affected by the nuclear explosions, the change in policy in this field has made it possible to surmount the difficulties created. Nevertheless, French specialized literature denotes some concern for the future in this connection, and it has been officially stressed that the role of France in the area is to maintain a balance.[20] As will be seen later, the need for this would seem to be correctly diagnosed. But what is questionable is whether a nation whose metropolis is so far away can really fulfill such a function at the present time.

Australia and New Zealand: South Pacific Powers

Australia and New Zealand are two other protagonists in the Pacific Islands area, of which, in a way, they too form a part. Although in specific aspects the policies pursued by these countries may differ, in their origins and in their broad outlines today they represent similar approaches. Both nations are the heirs of the British Empire in the region, not in a territorial sense but as regards the discharge of a role which the British withdrawal has left vacant. But this very heritage has made it somewhat difficult to formulate a policy towards the Pacific.

The fact that in both countries interest in the Pacific grew up in relation to their defense preoccupations[21] in itself involves a negative element. In the past this concern was reflected in pressure on the United Kingdom not to allow the occupation of the Pacific Islands by potentially antagonistic powers, such as France or Germany. Subsequently, keen anxiety began to be felt in relation to the Asian powers,[22] and this factor became preponderant in the foreign policies of Australia and New Zealand from the Second World War onwards, signs of a change having only recently appeared. In all these cases, as in that of the United States, relations with the Pacific stem from a strategic concern with policy towards Asia and not from an interest focussed on the area itself.

In 1944 Australia and New Zealand, under the Canberra Pact, sought to assume a preponderant and coordinated role in the Pacific Islands, but as matters turned out, the powers that won the war would not allow them to do so, and the colonial pattern was destined to continue almost unaltered.[23] In terms of defense, the two countries came to rely heavily on the United States and on the ANZUS system,[24] even becoming involved in the hostilities in Southeast Asia. The growing doubts as to the feasibility of this military alliance, which have been progressively gaining ground, suggest that once again the Pacific Islands will be viewed in a strategic perspective.

Despite the circumstance of geographical vicinity, a policy vis-à-vis the Pacific would often seem to be lacking.[25] This is partly imputable to the defense-oriented approach referred to, but partly also to the fact that Australia at least, as a continent, can aspire to a general international role and, in addition, to a role in the Indian Ocean, in Asia, and in the Pacific itself as a regional power. While this identification with the Pacific has been suggested as the most appropriate,[26] the prevailing trend seems to be towards closer cooperation with Asia, particularly with Japan, China, and ASEAN.[27] There can be no doubt that, politically and economically, cooperation with Asia is fully justified and has made it possible to dispel traditional apprehensions and introduce changes in the content of the foreign policy mentioned above.

Economic cooperation with the Pacific Islands is significant. In some cases it has been reflected in the establishment of special relations, like those existing between Australia and its former territory of Papua New Guinea, which involve substantial economic aid,[28] or between New Zealand and the self-governing Cook Islands. In other instances it is characterized by support for ad hoc projects, private investment flows, and other modalities.

Although Australia and New Zealand are the industrialized nations that are most integrated, geographically speaking, with the Pacific Islands, neither in intention nor in effect has this fact modified the trends towards nationalism and regional identification of this island community. Not even where special relations exist has the priority of the Pacific ceased to be the keynote of the political interest of the nations in question, as was seen in the case of Papua New Guinea. Thus, once again there is evidence to substantiate the statement made at the outset, to the effect that the Pacific Islands are identified only with their own geographical reality and their needs as developing countries.

The relations of the countries of ASEAN with the Pacific Islands are as yet in embryo, but their future potentialities should not be overlooked.[29] Until a short time ago these were developing countries whose international projection was limited by political upheavals and economic difficulties, a situation which hampered their linkage with the area in question. The economic success they have achieved, however, and the external projection of their economy, combined with greater political consolidation, have brought new and important relationships into being. These are maintained chiefly with Japan, China, and Australia, but they are already beginning to acquire importance in other spheres. Hence it may be hoped that in the future closer ties will be formed with the Pacific Islands, a move which would represent in addition a positive case of cooperation among developing countries.

Regional Agencies: Evolution towards Regional Autonomy

This broad framework constituted by the Pacific Islands' relations has also influenced the nature and evolution of international cooperation agencies in the region. In 1947 the Canberra Convention established the South Pacific Commission, of which the original members were all the administrating powers, i.e., the United States, France, the Netherlands,[30] the United Kingdom, Australia, and New Zealand. Furthermore, the South Pacific Conference was set up, which affords an opportunity for the member countries and territories of the region to meet once a year. Both agencies are still in existence, but as early as 1971 Fiji launched the initiative whereby the South Pacific Forum was created. Membership of the Forum is confined to the independent nations of the region—including Australia and New Zealand—and the quasi-independent countries like the Cook Islands. Thus dependent territories, as well as extraregional powers like the United States, France, and the United Kingdom, are excluded.

The South Pacific Forum clearly reflects the intention to possess political and economic cooperation mechanisms which will be representative of the regional identification and the new nationalist sentiment of the Pacific Islands. In this context, it is not impossible that in the future participation in the Forum may be confined exclusively to the Pacific Island nations as a grouping of developing countries. Within this framework has also been established the South Pacific Bureau for Economic Cooperation, which has promoted important projects.[31]

One of the principal projects recently considered was the signing of a Fishing Convention and the creation of a South Pacific Regional Fisheries Agency, in accordance with decisions adopted in 1977.[32] The objectives pursued by these mechanisms included the regulation of fishing for highly migratory species in the region in the light of the recent decisions of the United Nations Conference on the Law of the Sea. In addition to the countries that are members of the Forum, the United States, France, and the United Kingdom also participated in the negotiations, and various countries sent observers. Significantly, Chile was represented at these meetings; an interesting possibility is that the geographical area of the Convention might comprise Easter Island and other places under Chile's maritime jurisdiction in the Pacific.

Notwithstanding the importance of this project, the United States' fishing interests with respect to highly migratory species, especially tuna, led that country to oppose this initiative. Difficulties had already cropped up earlier between the United States and Micronesia on account of the latter's intention to apply a 200-mile exclusive zone.[33] All this was prejudicial to one of the most important interests of the Pacific Islands—as fishing is—entailing an almost exact recurrence of the problems that had arisen some decades before in Latin America's case in connection with the 200-mile zone which Chile promulgated in 1947 for the first time. This experience suggests that it would not be unlikely for the Pacific Islands to react in the future to the fishing operations of the United

States, Japan, the Soviet Union, and other countries with more drastic measures for the protection of their interests.

The evolution of the Pacific Islands has also had its repercussions on the United Nations mechanisms themselves. The former Economic Commission for Asia and the Far East was rebaptized as the Economic and Social Commission for Asia and the Pacific (ESCAP), a change which reflects the identity of the new region. These mechanisms are basically Asian, however, and the participation of the Pacific is still marginal.[34] Other agencies tend to assimilate the Pacific with Asia, despite the fact that no such identification exists in the region's political reality; cases in point are the Asian Development Bank and the Asian and Pacific Council (a Japanese initiative which has now lost its initial momentum). Most of the nongovernmental agencies also tend to group the Pacific with Asia.[35]

This raises the question of whether perhaps it would not be desirable for agencies concerned with the Pacific to be specific to that region, in the light of its own interests and identification, as is the case with the South Pacific Forum. Identification with Asia would not seem to be entirely appropriate. Still less justification is there for differentiating between the West and East Pacific, as some agencies do, since clearly the region is a single whole. The existence of its own agencies would not be designed to exclude the cooperation of Asia or of any other region or country, but, on the contrary, would facilitate access to new sources of cooperation, of which one might be Latin America itself. The sole significance of this orientation would be to recognize an existing reality and adapt cooperation to this reality and its specific needs.

The Constants of Traditional Relations

Within the framework of the international relations of the Pacific Islands certain constants can be seen which it is worthwhile to recapitulate, since they affect the prospects of a relationship with Latin America. The first outstanding fact is that traditionally the Pacific Islands have maintained active relations only with developed powers, either in Asia, in Europe, in America, or in Oceania, their linkage with the developing world being purely incipient.

The next point is that, as a general rule, none of these powers has envisaged its relations with the Pacific Islands as a function of their own merits and interests, but as part of a more complex relationship in which this region often figures as instrumental for the achievement of other aims. One of these objects has been defense strategy vis-à-vis Asia, another the possible establishment of a zone of influence, and yet another, to some extent, access to natural resources, especially those of the sea. This position certainly admits of exceptions, but it has been a frequently observable characteristic.

Hence the existing type of relations has been either of a colonial or of a paternalist character, a state of affairs which in neither case can last beyond a transition period.[36] The reaction of the Pacific Islands has already made itself clearly felt in the form of the emergence of an increasing island nationalism and regional identification which will exert every passing day a more decisive influence on the economic orientations, management of natural resources, nature and structure of the cooperation agencies, and participation in international organizations.

Notwithstanding this reaction, the weight that can be carried by the Pacific Islands' foreign policy is limited, especially in a geographical context in which the leading world powers are present. It is for this reason that the coordinator of interests and policies with other developing countries that share in the Pacific Basin may make a fundamental difference to the attainment of common objectives and introduce a necessary balance in the general framework of the international relations of the Pacific as a whole. Hitherto the region has been the scene of struggle and rivalry between major powers, whereby the Pacific Islands have been specifically affected. Things may be very different if perhaps this polarized system is transformed into a balanced relationship, to which the developing countries of the region can offer some important contributions.

Latin America and the Pacific Islands: Equilibrium, Cooperation, and Not Instrumentalization

Latin America is the continent which has been conspicuous by its absence in the Pacific, despite the important trans-Pacific links traceable in its history, and despite some significant efforts that have been made, though in the main sporadically.[37] Only in the course of the present decade have relations with Japan, China, Australia, and other countries begun to develop intensively, with a fundamentally economic emphasis which has, however, served to reintroduce the prospect of the presence of Latin America in the Pacific Basin.[38]

Everything seems to suggest that the participation of Latin America in the Pacific region as a broadly conceived whole will acquire steadily increasing importance. This is an aspect of the question which will be discussed later; for the moment it is of interest to consider how and to what extent this participation could be developed specifically with the Pacific Islands, in the light of the respective interests of both regions.

A first point that is worth stressing is that Latin America represents a real possibility for the Pacific Islands to initiate and maintain relations with developing countries within the ambit of the Pacific Basin, thus broadening the traditional pattern whereby they have kept up significant relations only with the developed powers in the area. The case of ASEAN also constitutes an interesting option which, as will be seen, is complementary to the link with Latin America.

Thus, the Pacific Islands, while diversifying their pattern of international relations, would forge a bond with countries like those of Latin America which share many of the economic and social problems besetting the nations of the Pacific, and which in other cases have had valuable experience in the course of the quest for appropriate solutions. While such a bond exists in a very general form at the level of the Group of 77 and other mechanisms, what might be desirable would be to make it effective at the level of much more specific cooperation, some elements of which will be mentioned later.

The second important aspect contributing to the viability of such a relationship between Latin America and the Pacific Islands is that since none of the Latin American countries is a developed power, it would be extremely unlikely that any of them might envisage its relations with the Pacific as the anteroom to relations with Asia or to an interest in that continent. Relations with Asia already exist and are conducted irrespectively of what this new system may be. Possibly they may be coordinated, but they could by no means come to represent a new instrumentalization of the

A Latin American Perspective

Pacific Islands, in line with what has been the historical constant up to now.

The recurrence of such a phenomenon is still more unlikely in Latin America's case, inasmuch as its relations with Asia and the Pacific are not based on any military, strategic, or defensive approach, such as is normally found to lie at the origin of this instrumentalization. Still less do racial considerations exist, which have sometimes influenced the attitude of certain countries towards Asia or the Pacific. Thus, Latin America would constitute virtually the first instance in which relations with the Pacific Islands were structured on the basis of the latter's own merits and interests and not with indirect aims. Cooperation, not instrumentalization, would be the basis of this relationship.

It must be borne in mind, however, that Latin America needs to act with caution in some aspects of its relations with Asia, so as not to be drawn into problems which are none of its concern and which might affect its relations with Asia and the Pacific as a whole. It is no exaggeration, for example, to surmise that in the future some Asian countries might look to some of the Latin American countries for military cooperation, taking into account the facts that Brazil has become a major exporter of arms, that Cuba has already established its presence in Asia, and even that Chile might possibly be called upon to counteract this Cuban penetration. Another example, already observable today, is the pressure on Latin America arising out of the problem of the refugees in Southeast Asia; while Latin America should not elude the humanitarian cause involved in this question, neither must the powers responsible for creating the situation excuse their own responsibility in finding a solution.

Insofar as relations with the Pacific Islands are grounded on principles and objectives that are compatible with the legitimate nationalism and growing identification of this region, they will be reflected in solid and lasting ties. The principles mentioned above in connection with a relationship with Latin America fully meet this requisite of compatibility, and therefore warrant very careful consideration of the best way of putting them into practice.

A probable consequence of the establishment and consolidation of firm relations between the Pacific Islands and Latin America would be the creation of conditions of balance in the sphere of trans-Pacific relations, insofar as these are connected with the interests of the South Pacific and with Latin America's interests in the Pacific region. If developing countries in the area were to coordinate their interests and policies, it would become very difficult for the traditional powers to impose their patterns and their desiderata on the region. A clear case in point is afforded by the resources of the ocean and the aforementioned project for the establishment of a regional fisheries agency. Would it have been possible for certain powers to have doomed it to failure if Latin America had taken part in the scheme, in view of the latter's past experience in this field and of the effective responses devised at the time? At least it would have been more difficult.

The contribution to equilibrium that such relations could make can also be assessed at another important level. Above it was noted that there have sometimes been signs of an intention to establish zones of influence in the Pacific Islands, and that this might lead to concerted policies on the part of the main poles of influence. Thus, the Pacific Islands as a region would continue to function as a "client" of the interested powers instead of on a footing of partnership or some similar mode of association. Relations with Latin America would enable this possibility to be averted, partly because they would offer alternatives that would serve as a buffer against such intentions, and partly because they would add some political weight to the presence of the Pacific Islands in the outside world.

The potential participation of ASEAN in this system of trans-Pacific linkage of the developing countries of the Pacific Basin would have a significant influence. The possibility of action open to each individual region—the Pacific Islands, Latin America, and ASEAN—is limited in the context of the huge Pacific Ocean. Concerted action on the part of two regions already introduces a different dimension, as has been discussed with respect to Latin America. An association of the whole group of developing countries would acquire a meaningful presence in the Pacific Basin to the advantage of all. In this sense, it would be highly desirable for the Pacific to be bridged on the basis of the regional trilogy of ASEAN, the Pacific Islands, and Latin America. To some extent Chile's policy towards the Pacific has already incorporated this three-fold dimension.[39] In terms of the structure of a Pacific community, an aspect which will be discussed later, this bridge of as-

A Latin American Perspective

sociation would be of still greater importance for coordinating the interests and activities of the developing countries in the framework of a major integration project like that of such a community.

Functional Interests in a Special Relationship: Towards a Council for the Pacific and Latin America

The bases on which a close relationship between the Pacific Islands and Latin America can be constructed are sound enough to guarantee the viability of the idea. Nevertheless, some concrete mechanisms must be identified whereby the idea can be put into effect. In this context, every possible effort ought to be made to shun formal institutional structures and, preferably, to encourage such modes of association as are related with specific functional interests. Once the latter have borne fruit the way may possibly be paved for more complex institutional structures to channel cooperation.

The first functional interest that stands out of itself is that of trade. It was previously pointed out that the Pacific Island countries are heavily dependent upon foreign trade and often show balance-of-payments problems. At this level, Latin America could perfectly well cooperate in the resolution of these problems by granting nonreciprocal trade preferences to the Pacific Islands. While it is true in respect of many items that the production of the latter region competes with Latin America's tropical production, for the countries of the southern zone of South America, at least, this problem would not arise. Chile has already announced in the United Nations Conference on Trade and Development its intention to grant concessions of this kind to the less-developed countries.

By establishing a trade flow,[40] Latin America too would benefit, since its exports to the Pacific Islands would increase to some extent, and in any case the two regions would acquire a knowledge of each other in the economic field which today is nonexistent. Such knowledge is the indispensable basis for the subsequent development of investment and other forms of economic cooperation.

The second functional interest which is also worth exploring is to be found on the plane of the transfer of technology. For the very reason that the Pacific Islands have traditionally been surrounded by industrial powers, access to technology has been hindered by the fact that the developed countries' supertechnology is inappropriate to the needs of the countries of the region. Latin America, on the other hand, could contribute an intermediate technology suitable to the requirements of developing countries. Similarly, it would be technology of this type that would normally accompany potential investment.[41]

Interests of another kind are to be found in the fields of transportation and communication. The pioneer work done in this connection by Lan-Chile with its Pacific route to Fiji might well be complemented by the plans of Air Pacific, in which Fiji is particularly interested. Trans-Antarctic flights likewise represent a potential development of relations in this field. The extension of these routes to Australia and Asia is also a desirable objective. Similarly, complementarity programs might be worked out for maritime transport.[42]

An area which is of special interest to both regions is that of utilization of the resources of the sea, in which close cooperation has already been initiated in the framework of the United Nations Conference on the Law of the Sea.[43] The first manifestation of this interest relates to fishing. Both the Pacific Island nations and the Latin American countries on the Pacific coast share a common concern for the conservation and rational utilization of these resources. In this connection the experience of Latin America, which began with the declaration of a 200-mile zone by Chile in 1947, is perfectly applicable to the Pacific Islands, a region which is beset by the same problems today. A possible coordination of policies between the two regions would enable them to control what are the richest fishing grounds in the world,[44] especially for tuna, and to subject the activities of third parties to well-established rules. The Permanent Commission for the Conservation and Exploitation of the Maritime Resources of the South Pacific, of which the members are Chile, Ecuador, and Peru, could perfectly well coordinate its action with that of the South Pacific Forum and its fisheries agency, Chile having already taken some steps in this direction.

Another manifestation of the interest under discussion will shortly be called forth by the question of utilization of the mineral resources of the seabed, of which the main deposits occur in the area outside the limits of national jurisdiction, their exploitation may affect the national economies, as in the event of an adverse economic impact on the countries which are land-based producers of the same minerals, which include Chile, Peru, Papua New Guinea, Fiji, and many others.[45] The location of processing plants, maritime pollution, and other aspects of the problem have similar repercussions. Fiji has expressed its interest in becoming the country where the Seabed Authority would have its headquarters.

Various other aspects of the Law of the Sea are of interest to both regions. They include archipelagic delimitation, the régime for the Islands, the régime for navigation through straits used for international navigation, and several others. In this last connection it must also be borne in mind that Latin American countries like Chile and Panama, and ASEAN countries like Indonesia and Singapore, control the principal means of access to the Pacific Ocean, such as the Panama Canal and the Straits of Magellan and of Malacca. Exchange of experience and coordination in this field would likewise be of great value.

The area of natural resources policy, with special emphasis on mining, is also highly important for cooperation between the Pacific Islands and Latin America. To some extent, this kind of cooperation has already been started through the Intergovernmental Council of Copper-Exporting Countries, of which Chile, Peru, Papua New Guinea, and Indonesia are members, as well as countries from other regions. The exchange of experience and coordination of policies in respect to copper and other minerals, such as iron, coal, and nickel, would be of great reciprocal benefit, particularly since the two regions possess substantial resources that are increasingly appreciated by the industrialized nations, several of which are potential members of the Pacific community.

Lastly, while not discounting other functional interests that might be mentioned, it is important to stress the enormous possibilities of reciprocal cooperation between the two regions on the basis of the existing institutions or of others which might perhaps be established. In the political sphere, for instance, while diplomatic missions are few, at the level of the United Nations there has been timely coordination, and cooperation has been successful. Nevertheless, increased cooperation will call for the strengthening of direct representation. The Chilean ambassador in New Zealand is accredited to all the Pacific Island countries. It would probably be desirable in the future for Chile to be represented in the Pacific

Islands by a mission in one of the countries which belong *stricto sensu* to this region.

Participation in one another's institutions could be another way of stimulating knowledge and cooperation, beginning with the presence of observers. In this connection, Chile has already participated in specific activities of the South Pacific Forum, as has been shown above. In the same way, why could not ESCAP and the United Nations Economic Commission for Latin America coordinate activities for the benefit of the Pacific Islands and Latin America? Other similar institutions might also take part in an effort of this kind, including those of a financial character such as the Inter-American Development Bank and the Asian Development Bank. The body of activities thus undertaken would constitute an authentic example of horizontal cooperation between developing countries.[46] Eventually this institutional network might lead to the establishment of a higher coordination organ such as a council for the Pacific and Latin America. Thus a new step would be taken towards the construction of a Pacific community.

Latin America, the Pacific Islands, and the Pacific Community

Since cooperation between the Pacific Islands and Latin America is feasible from the standpoint of the principles on which it could be based and the specific mechanisms through which it could operate, the question that remains is whether the will exists that could make this program possible. First and foremost, the initiative in approaching this cooperation must of course be taken by Latin America itself, as the relatively more developed region to which it is of interest to make its presence in the Pacific Basin more permanently felt. So far, as has already been pointed out, Chile is the country that has taken concrete steps in this direction.

Secondly, Latin America must be envisaged for these and other trans-Pacific cooperation purposes as a region in a broad sense, that is, not confined exclusively to the countries with an East Pacific coastline. Naturally the degree of participation in the process will depend upon each individual country's awareness and vocation. In this respect there is wide diversity in Latin America, for whereas in some cases a clearly formed consciousness of the possibilities is observable, in others it is absolutely lacking or exists only in relation to specific ends, such as cooperation with the industrial powers of the Pacific. The process is one which will certainly require maturing, but which can be very effectively started already, and in connection with which specific examples of cooperation have been mentioned.

A third consideration is of supreme importance. As was remarked before, relations between the Pacific Islands and Latin America would be complementary to the latter's relations throughout the broad Pacific Ocean, and in no way would there be substitution. In this sense, the relationship in question should be envisaged as part of a broader Pacific community,[47] in which it is incorporated, and in the construction of which it represents a step. A similar relationship with ASEAN is likewise conceivable.

Such a prospect, however, is not altogether clear in the sight of the major Pacific powers, which do not yet visualize Latin American participation in the Pacific Basin or in a future Pacific community. A decade ago, for example, the prime minister of Japan defined as a foreign policy objective the concept of "Asia-Pacific,"[48] essentially based on the Asian and Pacific Council, which was a geographically restricted system. Round about the same time, high officials of the State Department expressly excluded Latin America from the Pacific system.[49] This was understandable ten years ago, but it is frankly incomprehensible that today, directly or indirectly, a view which is no longer in touch with reality should be reaffirmed.

In 1979, in fact, the prime minister of Japan, on an important occasion, only mentioned Latin America in passing and without linking it up with the Pacific.[50] On the same occasion, Japan's foreign minister classed relations with Latin America on the same level as those with Africa.[51] Another high official of the State Department, referring to the political prospects of the Pacific Basin, omitted all mention of Latin America.[52] The president of the Pacific Basin Economic Council, a high executive of the Chamber of Commerce and Industry of Tokyo, had maintained shortly before that to include East Pacific countries in the concept of a Pacific Ocean economic zone was going too far.[53]

This attitude is an obstacle which Latin America will have to surmount in its process of linkage with the Pacific, both by becoming Pacific-conscious itself and by inducing other nations to perceive a Latin American role in the Pacific Basin. This is desirable not only for Latin America but also for the concept of a Pacific community, which would be markedly strengthened by the incorporation of an immense continent. It is encouraging to note that some analysts have already appreciated this new dimension.[54]

Ten years ago, Sir Keith J. Holyoake, then prime minister and today governor-general of New Zealand, concluded an article noteworthy for its foresight with the following remarks: "It is certain that Latin America's presence will be increasingly felt throughout the Pacific. It is a continent of enormous potential, which by the end of this century will have twice the population of the United States and Canada put together. It is also a continent whose present problems, political, economic, and social, can only be described as gigantic.[55] The presence of Latin America in the Pacific will be the outcome not only of its will and vocation, but also of its own skill in resolving those problems, which are still affecting it today.

NOTES

1. John P. Craven, *Tropical Oceania: The Newest World*, mimeographed text (Hawaii: Steel Service Center Institute, 1977).
2. See, for example, the manifesto of the Banabans, former inhabitants of Ocean Island and living today in Fiji, in favor of that island's independence of the Gilbert Islands or its association with Fiji, and protests of an economic order on account of the exploitation of phosphates. See "The Banabans: Historical Background and recent development," *Australian Foreign Affairs Record*, June 1977, pp. 319-322. For other examples connected with the process of independence of Papua New Guinea, see Ralph R. Prendas, "Secessionist politics in Papua New Guinea," *Pacific Affairs*, Spring 1977, pp. 64-85.
3. Quoted in "Development of Papua New Guinea's foreign relations," *Australian Foreign Affairs Record*, April 1977, p. 187. See also James Byth, "Niugini: una nueva nación cuprífera en el Pacífico se acerca a su independencia," *Estudios Internacionales*, no. 22 (April-June 1973), pp. 82-105.
4. The Hon. Tupuola Efi, "Statement by Prime Minister of Western Samoa on small states," Commonwealth Heads of Government Regional Meeting, Sydney, 13-16 February 1978, *Australian Foreign Affairs Record*, February 1978 (supplement), p. 40.
5. For an analysis of United States policy, see R. A. Herr, "Jimmy Carter and American Foreign Policy in the Pacific Islands,"*Australian Outlook*, August 1978, pp. 224-238.
6. See Eugene B. Mikaly, "La estrategia de los Estados Unidos en el Pacífico

Occidental y el dilema de Micronesia," *Estudios Internacionales*, no. 17 (January–March 1972), pp. 25–39.
7. See, in general, Barbara Johnson and Frank Langdon, "The Impact of the Law of the Sea Conference upon the Pacific Region: Part I," *Pacific Affairs*, Spring 1978, pp. 5–23; and ibid., "Part II," Summer 1978, pp. 216–229.
8. Herr, p. 238.
9. For an analysis of the presence of the Soviet Union in the Pacific in general, see Ernst Kux, "Is Russia a Pacific Power?," *Pacific Community*, April 1970, pp. 498–510.
10. Herr, p. 231.
11. For an analysis of strategic factors in the area, see T. B. Miller, "The Indian and Pacific Oceans: some strategic considerations," *Adelphi Papers*, no. 57, (May 1969); Hedley Bull, "The new balance of power in Asia and the Pacific," *Foreign Affairs*, July 1971, pp. 669–681; Obaid ul haq, "The changing balance of power in the Pacific and its implications for Southeast Asia: a possible scenario," *Pacific Community*, April 1975, pp. 378–392; Paul Dibb, "The strategic interrelations of the United States, the USSR and China in the East Asia-Pacific area," *Australian Outlook*, August 1978, pp. 169–181. See also Pacific Forum, *Future Economic and Security Cooperation in the Pacific Region* (Hawaii, 1979).
12. See Anthony Haas, "The South Pacific and Japan," *Pacific Community*, April 1975, pp. 435–451. See also, "Papua New Guinea-Japan: Mr. Somare's visit," *Australian Foreign Affairs Record*, December 1977, pp. 627–628.
13. Among the waters with the highest fishing potential in the world are to be found, precisely, those of the Southeast Pacific and the central South Pacific. See Sidney Holt, "Marine Fisheries," *Ocean Yearbook 1* (Chicago: University of Chicago Press), pp. 35–83.
14. For an analysis of relations between Japan and each of the Pacific Island nations, see A. Haas.
15. Eisaku Sato, "Pacific Asia," *Pacific Community*, October 1969, pp. 1–3.
16. For relations between Australia and Japan, see T. B. Millar, "Japan and Australia: partners in the Pacific," *Pacific Community*, October 1976, pp. 28–42.
17. Fiji, Nauru, Papua New Guinea, Tonga, and Western Samoa are members of the Commonwealth. See "Communiqué: Commonwealth Heads of Government Regional Meeting," *Australian Foreign Affairs Record*, February 1978 (supplement), pp. 8–15.
18. Pierre Chaussan, "La France dans le Pacifique," *Défense Nationale*, July 1978, pp. 69–77.
19. René Chiroux, "Les Nouvelles-Hébrides sur le chemin de l'indépendance: nouvelles menaces dans l' océan Pacifique?," *Défense Nationale*, January 1979, pp. 35–47.
20. See the statement made by Jacques Chirac during his visit to French Polynesia in July 1978: "If France were no longer present, the Pacific, and in particular the South Pacific, would be like a vast American-Japanese

lake. Our role in this region is one of maintaining equilibrium. It is no concern of ours to dispute the place held on the strategic level and on the economic level by the United States, Japan, and Australia. Our concern is to contribute the wealth of our culture and a reflection of our conception of the world and of international relations. As a counterpart, the Pacific territories are for France one of the irreplaceable elements of its diversity and its dimension," (unofficial translation) *Nouvelles de Tahiti*, 20 July 1978. Quoted by René Chiroux, p. 46.

21. Bruce Grant, "Australia y el Pacífico," *Estudios Internacionales*, no. 17 (January–March 1972), pp. 40–52.
22. C. Hartley Grattan, "Perspectives on Australian Foreign Policy," *Pacific Affairs*, Spring 1975, pp. 87–93.
23. Keith J. Holyoake, "A new role for New Zealand in the Pacific," *Pacific Community*, April 1970, pp. 369–381, especially p. 379.
24. Hugh Collins, "Australia and the United States: assessing the relationship," *Australian Outlook*, August 1978, pp. 153–168; and Henry S. Albinsk, "American Perspectives on the ANZUS alliance," *Australian Outlook*, August 1978, pp. 131–152.
25. See, for example, an article by the leader of the opposition in the Australian Federal Parliament, the Hon. W. G. Hayden, "Australian Foreign Policy: Morality and Reality," *Australian Outlook*, April 1978, pp. 3–15. In this article no reference is made to the Pacific Islands, except for Papua New Guinea.
26. See B. Grant. Also W. Macmahon Ball, "Australia en el Pacífico," Estudios Internacionales, no. 20 (October–December 1972), pp. 40–52.
27. See "ASEAN-Australia economic co-operation," *Australian Foreign Affairs Record*, November 1977, pp. 590–593. Also T. B. Millar.
28. See J. D. Stevenson and N. D. Karunaratne, "The need and criteria for the sectoral programing of Australian aid to Papua New Guinea," *The Development Economies*, June 1978, pp. 123–146.
29. See "Regionalism in South-East Asia: the ASEAN experience," *Australian Foreign Affairs Record*, June 1978, pp. 290–295.
30. The Netherlands withdrew in 1964 on the grounds of not possessing territories in the region. See Chaussan, pp. 71–73.
31. Some writers have seen in these initiatives the emergence of a regional nationalism directed against the extra-regional powers. See Chaussan, p. 73.
32. See the Declaration on the Law of the Sea and the Regional Fisheries Agency adopted by the Eighth South Pacific Forum, Port Moresby, 31 August 1977, in *Australian Foreign Affairs Record*, September 1977, pp. 468–470. See also *Australian Foreign Affairs Record*, December 1977, p. 632.
33. Herr, p. 229.
34. For the work of this agency, see "Development through co-operation: the work of the Economic and Social Commission (ESCAP)," *Australian Foreign Affairs Record*, July 1977, pp. 336–343.
35. For a list of nongovernmental agencies in the Pacific region, see George S. Kanahele and Michael Haas, "Prospects for a Pacific Community," *Pacific Community*, October 1974, pp. 83–93, especially pp. 88–89.
36. Reference has also been made to neocolonial situations. See, for example,

A Latin American Perspective

Ralph Pettman, "The Solomon Islands: a developing neo-colony?," *Australian Outlook*, August 1977, pp. 268-278.

37. Government undertakings have generally aimed at serving commercial ends. Those of an academic order have been of a broader scope. Among the latter, the Institute of International Studies of the University of Chile has played a pioneer role with the following conferences and seminars: (1) América Latina vuelve al Pacífico (Latin America returns to the Pacific) (Viña del Mar, 1970); (2) Ciencia y Tecnología en la Cuenca del Pacífico (Science and Technology in the Pacific Basin) (Viña del Mar, 1975); (3) La Comunidad del Pacífico: hacia un rol para América Latina (The Pacific Community: towards a role for Latin America) (Easter Island, 1979). Similarly, in 1978-1979 the Institute organized an interdisciplinary study group on relations between Latin America and the Pacific, which led to the establishment of a study area.

    The following publications are connected with these activities: Francisco Orrego Vicuña, "Chile en el Pacífico," *Revista Portada*, no. 43, December 1973; Francisco Orrego Vicuña, *El Océano Pacífico*, Santiago, Chile, Editorial Gabriela Mistral, 1975; Francisco Orrego Vicuña (ed.), *Ciencia y Tecnología en la Cuenca del Pacífico*, Santiago, Chile, Instituto de Estudios Internacionales, 1976. Two other works are in preparation under the direction of the same author: "Las Relaciones entre América Latina y la región Asia-Pacífico"; and "América Latina en la Comunidad del Pacífico."

38. On relations with Japan, see Gustavo Andrade, "Japón y América Latina: una relación en continuo cambio," with China, see Walter Sánchez, "La creciente presencia internacional de China y su impacto en la región Asia-Pacífico," with other countries, see Javier Illanez, "El rol internacional de la India y su efecto en la relación transpacífico al nivel de países en desarrollo," and on the economic emphasis, see Juan Reutter, "Diagnóstico y perspectivas de las relaciones económicas entre la región Asia-Pacífico y América Latina," all publications of the Instituto de Estudios Internacionales, Study Group on the Asia-Pacific region, 1979.

39. In addition to relations with the South Pacific, diplomatic and economic ties with ASEAN have recently begun to be intensified. The vice-minister for foreign affairs of Chile, Enrique Valdés Puga, paid an official visit to the ASEAN countries in May 1979.

40. Trade statistics show that the Pacific Islands do not export to Latin America. Latin America in its turn, exports only three million dollars to the Pacific Islands. See J. Reutter.

41. Generally speaking, the Pacific Islands have displayed interest in investment in manufactures with a view to adopting an export policy like that of Singapore. This would permit significant Latin American participation in industry of this type.

42. Under the sponsorship of the South Pacific Forum the South Pacific Regional Shipping Council has been established, as well as a new shipping line, the Pacific Forum Line. See *Australian Foreign Affairs Record*, March 1977, p. 158.

43. See Johnson and Langdon.

44. The 200-mile Exclusive Economic Zone of the Pacific Island countries represents an area of 6 million square miles. See J. Reutter.
45. See Francisco Orrego Vicuña, *Los Fondos Marinos y Oceánicos*, Santiago, Chile, Editorial Andrés Bello, 1976.
46. The Commonwealth Heads of Government of the Asian region and of the Pacific "called on the international community to give greater recognition to the special problems of these countries and to grant special measures, which would give added impetus to their economic and social development, and to promote further co-operation and progress in the area." See Communiqué, pp. 9-10. The horizontal cooperation mentioned and that of the agencies for both regions would be in keeping with this policy.
47. See, in general, Kanahele and Haas.
48. See Sato; see also Robert Guillian, "A New Pacific Age," *Pacific Community*, April 1970, pp. 487-497.
49. See U. Alexis Johnson, "The Pacific Basin," *Pacific Community*, October 1969, pp. 11-19, especially p. 14.
50. Policy Speech by Prime Minister Masayoshi Ohira at the 87th Session of the National Diet, 25 January 1979, Japan, Foreign Press Center, mimeographed text, p. 8.
51. Foreign policy speech by Sunao Sonoda, minister for foreign affairs, Japan, Foreign Press Center, mimeographed text, p. 7.
52. Address by The Hon. David D. Newsom, undersecretary of state for political affairs, before the Pacific Basin Economic Council, Los Angeles, California, May 15, 1979, in *Political Perspectives in the Pacific Basin*, Department of State Press, May 15, 1979, no. 132.
53. See Noborn Goto, "Pacific Basin Gaining Recognition," ASEAN and I (10), *Mainichi Daily News*, 14 August 1978. Apparently the scope of this reference to an economic area is different from that of the proposition regarding a free trade area. On the latter, see Kiyoshi Kojima, "Un área de libre comercio del Pacífico," *Estudios Internacionales*, no. 20 (October-December 1972), pp. 53-66.
54. See, for example, Jiro Tokuyama, "Opening of Pacific Century," *Look Japan*, January 10, 1979. This writer considers that as from the mid-1980s a consolidated Pacific community, including Latin America, will be clearly in sight.
55. See Keith J. Holyoake, p. 381.

Changing Patterns of Trade and Trends in Trade Policy in the Asia-Pacific Region
Nam Duck-Woo

Nam Duck-Woo, an academic economist, has long served in a variety of major government posts in the Republic of Korea. He is presently prime minister. His paper details the perspective of many in Korea and the other newly industrialized powers of East Asia with respect to greater regional cooperation. In general, there is a shared view that policies supporting free and unfettered trade lie at the core of all successful development strategies and, correspondingly, that any viable plan for regional organization must be similarly founded. The paper delineates this view with considerable detail and conviction. In the process, it also chides the United States and Japan for failing to provide strong leadership on behalf of open trading arrangements and reminds both that their own economic interests are best served by such arrangements. The United States in particular is criticized for yielding to the blandishments of protectionism during the past decade and is warned that it cannot expect to regain its earlier economic vitality unless its present course is altered.

Introduction

The concept of a Pacific community has received increasing attention in recent years. It has been the topic of numerous discussions and conferences within the academic and business communities on both sides of the Pacific Ocean. On the level of government, a subcommittee of the United States Congress has determined to "take it [the idea] out of the ivory tower" for its own deliberation, while in Japan the prime minister formed a study group devoted to a full examination of the issues and the further development of the idea.

The Pacific community concept was first aired in Japan as

early as 1965 by Professor Kiyoshi Kojima and echoed later by Australian scholars. Kojima's proposal, however, went largely unheeded for more than a decade, although there was an undercurrent of smaller-scale regional organizational activity during this period as exemplified by the formation of the Pacific Basin Economic Council in 1967, the Pacific Trade and Development Conferences in 1968, and, the most important, the Association of South East Asian Nations (ASEAN) in 1967.

What then are the major factors behind the revival of the concept of the Pacific community? Some commentators are impressed by the heightened role of the Asia-Pacific region in the world economy; others stress the growing interdependence among the countries in the region; and there are still others who, in broad and long-term historical perspective, maintain that in the sequence of the development of world history the center of gravity is bound to shift from the Atlantic to the Asia-Pacific region, not only in terms of economics but also politics and culture.

Meanwhile, Hugh Patrick, Peter Drysdale, and Lawrence Krause have pointed out three factors responsible for giving impetus to the increased importance of the Pacific within the world economy and the growth of economic interdependence among the Asia-Pacific economies themselves: (1) the growth of Japan's industrial power, (2) the remarkable trade and industrial growth of developing economies of Northeast and Southeast Asia, and finally (3) the slide towards slower growth in Western Europe.

It is evident that the revival of the idea of organizing a Pacific community is a reflection of the changing economic realities for countries in the region and their growing interdependent relationship. These realities may be studied in such terms as economic growth, trade, investment, and finance resources. This paper, however, is an examination of the major characteristics of changing patterns of trade in the Asia-Pacific region and their relationship to the evolving concept of the Pacific community as regards the issue of trade policy as an effective means of international cooperation.

The Asia-Pacific region is a geographically ambiguous term. In this study, it is rather narrowly defined to cover the region's five industrial countries: The United States, Canada, Japan, Australia, and New Zealand; three Northeast Asian countries: Taiwan, Hong Kong, and South Korea; and the five ASEAN nations:

Indonesia, Malaysia, Singapore, the Philippines, and Thailand. These thirteen countries constitute the major part of the Asia-Pacific region however the term is defined.

The Asia-Pacific Region in World Trade

Over the eighteen-year period extending from 1960 to 1978, world exports increased approximately ninefold from a level of US$130 billion to US$1,190 billion in current prices. Taking account of the change in the index of the unit value of world exports which increased from 40 in 1960 to 123 in 1978 (1975 = 100), it is safe to say that world exports in real terms increased about three times over the same period. This rapid expansion of international trade coupled with an equally high growth in world output has often been described as a world economic boom greater than that of any previous period in history.

The Asia-Pacific region has played a major role in the expansion of world trade. The combined exports of the thirteen countries in the region increased about ten times from a level of US$38 billion in 1960 to US$381 billion in 1978, signifying that trade expansion in the Asia-Pacific region advanced even more rapidly than elsewhere in the world. The combined share of the Asia-Pacific countries in world exports increased from 28 percent in 1960 to 32 percent in 1978.

As elsewhere, Asia-Pacific exports experienced setbacks during the 1970s relative to the 1960s. This reflects the adverse turn of the international economic environment in recent years. These setbacks have been characterized by the recurrence of international monetary instability, spread of protectionism in the developed countries, upsurge of petroleum prices, protracted economic stagnation coupled with chronic inflation and imbalance in the balance of payments in both developed and oil-importing developing countries, and so on. The average annual growth rate of exports of the five industrialized countries dropped from 8.9 percent in real terms for the 1960s to 5.4 percent for the 1970s (1970–1978). That of the three semi-industrialized countries dropped from 24 to 18 percent, while the ASEAN countries achieved an exceptional 7.9 percent growth rate in the 1970s compared with 4.2 percent in the previous decade. In balance, the export performance of the Asia-Pacific area as a whole fared better than the rest of the world.

The growth rate for the industrialized countries in the region remained comparable to that of European counterparts. In developing areas, exports continued to grow at a marked contrast to the rest of the developing world where at least thirty-eight countries experienced negative growth rates during the 1970-1977 period.

Changing Position of the U.S. in World Trade

Perhaps the most significant development in the two decades following World War II is in the relative decline of the American position in the world economy, particularly as it relates to Japan. In 1960 Japan's Gross Domestic Product (GDP) stood at less than one-tenth that of the United States, but in 1978 Japan's GDP was about one-half that of the United States. Consequently, Japan has become the second largest economic power in the free world. The two countries' changing relationship in world trade is equally striking. In 1960 the total American export to the world (US$20.6 billion) was five times as large as that of Japan (US$4.1 billion), but in 1978 the difference had slipped to less than 32 percent (US$144 billion versus US$98 billion).

The relative decline of the American position is indicated by steadily diminishing share in world exports since the mid-1960s. It decreased from 15.6 percent in 1960 to 14.8 percent in 1970 and to 11.6 percent in 1978. By contrast, Japan's share has risen steadily from 3.1 percent in 1960 to 6.6 percent in 1970 and to 8.0 percent in 1978. It is revealing to compare the changing pattern of geographical distribution of exports of the two countries among the six regional groupings of the world: Asia-Pacific, the European Economic Community (EEC), the oil-producing countries, the other countries of the Western Hemisphere, Africa, and the communist countries including the Soviet Union and mainland China. The distributional share of American exports decreased in all these regions between 1970 and 1978, with the exception of the oil-producing countries and the communist countries, whereas Japanese exports increased in all cases except Asia-Pacific and Africa.

It is noteworthy that Japan, a resource-poor nation, has been more successful than the United States in export-market expansion and that this success in market diversification is partly due to her political position—she had few or no political barriers in conducting trade with other nations throughout the world. In contrast, because of its international political role, the United States chose to limit or deny trade with such adversaries as Iran, Cuba, Indochina, and the Soviet Union. Perhaps reflecting these circumstances, Japan's exports to the oil-producing countries grew faster than those of the United States between 1970 and 1978, and Japan's exports to the communist bloc surpassed those of the United States in absolute amounts in 1978 (US$6 billion versus US$4 billion).

The relative setback of the United States in the world market presents a case for it to turn its economic attention to the Asia-Pacific region, an area where its concerns and priorities thus far have been focused primarily on military security problems. The Pacific economy provides an import market for industrial goods, agricultural products, and raw materials. In 1978 the region as a whole accounted for about 39 percent of the total exports and 47 percent of the imports of the United States. Asian-Pacific countries also provide a significant outlet for direct investment for American firms and for its financial capital flows. American investment in the region accounted for about one-quarter of the accumulated foreign investment at the end of 1978. The United States has been playing a major role in the Pacific as the largest provider of private and official capital and technology and has made great contributions to the development of the region. However, even here there has been a relative decline in its position. In terms of trade, the Asia-Pacific countries as a group accounted for roughly 41 percent of America's exports in 1970, but the proportion decreased to 39 percent in 1978, and the United States is now second to Japan in the amount of direct investment in the region.

Economically speaking, there is nothing inherently wrong with the relative decline in the American share of world trade. It is merely a reflection of the economic advancement of Japan and a number of developing countries, a process supported by American foreign policy in the postwar period. In general, one can hypothesize that the global share of trade between the developed and developing countries is bound to change over time in favor of the latter if the international effort to reduce the income gap between the two camps is truly successful and if international trade is a major mechanism through which economic growth can be transmitted. Nor does the relative decline in the trade share imply that the American people have become worse off. Although the United

States has been, and still is, the single largest trading nation in the world, its dependence on trade for economic growth is limited as indicated by the low ratio of exports and imports to Gross National Product (GNP) which stood at 6 percent in 1978. However, this is not to imply that trade does not contribute to the well-being of the people. Making suitable foreign products available at low prices is the very foundation of the economic rationale of foreign trade. Indeed, this has been noted with concern by some American writers, mainly because of its implications for the nation's economic and strategic interests in a global context.

Concern has been expressed by American writers in recent years over the country's diminishing role in preserving a liberal international trade system which promotes free, multinational flows of goods, services, and capital. One of the best examples is the recent report titled "An Asian-Pacific Regional Economic Organization: An Exploratory Concept Paper" prepared by Professors Hugh Patrick and Peter Drysdale for the Committee on Foreign Relations of the United States Senate. The report explicitly states that:

> While the Pacific economy has become a more significant component of the American interests, U.S. influence is declining because of the reduced relative importance of its trade and investment to the Western Pacific countries . . . in our view serious consideration is warranted of a foreign economic policy objective of developing a framework within which this evolving change of the United States' relative economic power is both more manageable and more productive of benefits to the United States.

Since one of the United States' major concerns is professed to be the preservation and extension of open and competitive relations in trade, investment, and finance, let us briefly review the evolution of American commercial policy in the post–World War II period. Historically, there has been a firm commitment to the notion that the national economic welfare is best served by free international trade and to the idea that any tariff reduction should be uniform in accordance with the most favored nation principle. Such a policy is reflected in the Reciprocal Trade Agreement Act of 1934 and the Trade Expansion Act of 1962, the act which formed the basis for the Kennedy round of tariff negotiations. The success of these negotiations is reflected in the estimate that the average *ad valorem* tariff on imports into the United States was reduced from 50 percent in 1945 to about 8 percent in 1967 when the Kennedy round was completed. The United States has been a leading member of the International Monetary Fund and a semiofficial member of the General Agreement on Tariffs and Trade (GATT), organizations designed to promote international trade. In international investment, American foreign investment has been encouraged with special tax provisions, an insurance system, bilateral treaties on the avoidance of double taxation, navigation aid, sanctions against nations that expropriate American property (Hickenlooper Amendments), and special loans to firms in less-developed countries that take on American partners (the Cooly loans).

The American posture on liberal trade and investment has obviously been strengthened by the economic advantages the nation gained from free trade during the postwar years when it was unquestionably the largest, most technologically advanced, and most productive power in the world. However, as the nation's economic leadership role began to decline in the 1960s, so did its concern for the promotion of free trade and investments. The Trade Act of 1974 marks a turning point in this regard. Most important, it adopted for the first time in forty years the concept of *conditional* most favored nation status. This means that concessions will be granted only to those countries who reciprocate, whereas in the past tariff cuts applied uniformly to all countries. Second, in the negotiation of codes on nontariff barriers, Congress encouraged the executive branch to make advantages available only to countries signing such agreements.

It is unfair to say that the move away from the most favored nation principle was led solely by the United States. The principle was breached when the EEC was formed, although the United States supported the move for various reasons, including its own multinational investment activities in Western Europe. Other preferential trading areas such as the Andean Pact and the Central American Common Market were also created. As a result, bilateral quotas, voluntary restraints on exports, countervailing duties, and import surcharges have become familiar expressions in the United States. How far the government will resist the protectionist impulse is a matter of concern not only for American economists but also for many other countries, particularly the developing countries as they are most affected by protectionism. As to future prospects and hopes, we must reserve judgment until we have observed the scene outside of the United States.

The Rise of Japan's Economy

Japan's economic interest in the Pacific region is more real and greater than that of any country in the area. In Sir John Crawford's words, "Japan is in no position to function, let alone continue to grow, without trade for food, energy, and raw materials with the region." In 1978, about 25 percent of Japan's exports went to developing countries in the Asia-Pacific region. In terms of her export market, this region is second only to the United States (27 percent) followed by the Middle East and the EEC. In terms of her import market, Japan depends on the Asia-Pacific region for 34 percent of her food, 36 percent of her raw materials, 20 percent of her minerals and fuels, and 23 percent of her manufactured goods. It is no accident that the most positive interest in the concept of a Pacific community has been shown by Japanese writers.

As indicated by numerous writings in recent years, Japanese views on trade with the Asia-Pacific region are largely based upon the following considerations: First, many Japanese writers are of the opinion that the vigor of the Western European economy has generally been lost with the economic integration of the region, and therefore no further stimulus is likely to spill over into the Japanese economy. They also believe that Japan cannot expect much economic stimulus from the implementation of the Tokyo round of multilateral tariff negotiations under the GATT because the result of the negotiations, overshadowed by the heightening of protectionism that took place in the meantime, was far below that of the Kennedy round.

Second, Professor Kojima observed that the United States, by diffusing its technology too quickly throughout the world and by engaging in hasty multinational direct investments during the postwar period, has weakened its economic position in the world. In his view, the decade of the 1970s produced a deadlock in many fields. To overcome such deadlocks, it is essential that a new development center for the world economy be created. The most promising locale for such a center is among the fast-developing countries of Asia and the Pacific.

Finally, surprising as it may be to American readers, many Japanese writers believe that the United States and the EEC are prone to protectionism because they are much less dependent on trade than Japan, and therefore their trade policies are more easily swayed by considerations of domestic interest. In the Japanese view it is of utmost importance that the nation seek potential markets elsewhere in order to continue her vital export growth.

Japanese views on trade with other Asian countries are based on the following analysis: (1) Japan's exports are not concentrated in a few items but diverse enough to meet the demand of any country or region; (2) the composition of Japanese exports is competitive with that of Northeast Asian countries, but exports from these countries have been growing rapidly due to the recent dynamic growth of their economies; (3) the ASEAN and the South Pacific countries present no challenge to Japanese exports because Japan's export composition is complementary to that of these countries, and her exports to them are expected to grow as they make continuous industrial progress on the basis of their large growth potential; and (4) Japan's industrial structure is flexible enough to adapt itself to both vertical and horizontal specialization as the need arises.

In promoting their trade interests with Asian countries, Japanese writers invariably stress the importance of liberalization of trade among the countries in the region. The following passage illustrates:

> Japan, unlike the USA and the EEC, has no choice but to pursue free-trade policies, in view of her particular economic circumstances. Even if other Western powers all run into frantic protectionism, Japan must adhere to the policy of liberal trade, at least in the Asian region. It is for this simple reason that, as long as smooth trade flows are maintained between Japan and the region, Japan's economic foundation will remain firm.

Under present circumstances, free-trade policy on the part of industrialized countries calls for industrial adjustment, giving ground to the developing-country exports based on more efficiency-oriented, labor-intensive production. Such adjustment, however, has not been easy primarily because of mounting resistance from competing industries in the industrialized countries which are troubled by the disruption and the displacement of jobs.

Although they are well aware of this problem, Japanese writers stress that Japan must meet this challenge in order to maintain her leadership in the region and to prove her capability of carrying out the needed adjustment. Given the size and resilience of the Japanese economy, they observe, a marginal adjustment on the part of Japan would be sufficient to encourage an overall positive adjustment on the part of developing countries. This, in turn, would enhance specialization in the area of comparative advantages which would increase the level of income of the developing countries.

The confidence of Japanese writers in free trade obviously stems from the great degree of Japan's economic maturity. In terms of export structure, Japan has already achieved a high degree of industrial adjustment in response to changing circumstances. For example, between 1960 and 1976 the percentage of her total manufactured exports represented by textiles and clothing fell from 28 percent to only 6 percent, while that of machines and transportation equipment rose from 23 to 53 percent and that of other manufactured goods rose from 28 to 37 percent. As regards imports, Japan's purchase abroad is heavily skewed toward fuel and other primary products such as foodstuff and minerals, goods which comprised about 65 percent of her total imports in 1976. The purchase of manufactured goods, on the other hand, accounted for only 18 percent in the same year. Therefore, Japan presently has little reason to fear foreign competition either at home or abroad in terms of its general impact on her economy.

The Emergence of Newly Industrializing Countries

The four newly industrializing countries of Asia—Taiwan, Hong Kong, Singapore, and South Korea—have attracted much attention in recent years because of the rapid growth of their economies and the even more rapid expansion of their exports to the industrialized countries of the Asia-Pacific region and Western

Europe. The expansion of labor-intensive light-industrial exports such as textiles, clothing, shoes, and electronic gadgets has had a considerable impact on competing industries in the developed countries. As a consequence, a series of import restrictions in various forms ensued in a number of industrialized countries. For example, in the early 1970s the United States had over twenty bilateral agreements with individual countries limiting textile imports. It is estimated that four types of nontariff barriers alone—quotas, variable levies, voluntary restraints, and licensing—affected approximately one-third (by value) of the exports from non-oil-producing developing countries in 1974. In 1976 the Generalized System of Preferences was put into effect by the United States and the other industrialized countries. It grants duty-free treatment to developing-country exports if certain criteria are met. Unfortunately, there were notable exceptions. Such major exports from the Pacific developing countries as shoes, textiles, and some sensitive electric and steel products did not receive preferential treatment.

Caught between the restrictive pressure from the industrialized countries and the progress of the less-developed countries in the export of labor-intensive products, the newly industrializing countries attempted to find a way out by moving toward more capital-intensive and skill-oriented production. The reaction to this from the industrialized countries was that they were affected by the so-called boomerang effect, the idea that the supply of capital and technology to developing countries had brought about a negative return to the supplying country in terms of its share in the world export market and employment in its import-competing industries—an argument that warrants no further comment.

Unfortunately, the impact of the economic advancement of the newly industrializing countries has been exaggerated, and the arguments for import restrictions against the products of these countries are not economically well founded. In the first place, impressive as the growth of exports from these countries may have been, the share taken by any particular nation in the world export market is still around 1 percent (0.9 percent for Hong Kong, 1.02 percent for Korea, 1.03 percent for Taiwan, and 0.8 percent for Singapore). Further, the impact of these exports on industrial-power domestic markets is almost negligible. They ranged from 1 percent of total American imports in the case of Singapore to 3.2 percent in the case of Taiwan. The comparable figures for Japan varied from 0.4 percent for Singapore to 2.5 for Korea.

Next, much of the impetus for import restrictions against the exports of the newly industrializing countries stems from the concern over the domestic employment effects of trade with developing countries. However, this concern usually overlooks the fact that while imports from developing countries may displace jobs in the import-competitive industries, exports to developing countries create jobs in the exporting sector of the economy. It must be remembered that developing countries have always imported more from developed countries than they have exported and that the resulting trade deficits have always been covered by the borrowings from the developed countries. Without an adequate increase in their exports, there is no way for the developing countries to pay back their foreign debts.

A number of analyses on employment effects have been carried out, including studies for the United States and the Organization for Economic Cooperation and Development. A World Bank report concluded that estimates of employment effects range from negligible to a small net loss. Moreover, these studies have shown that "the employment implication of imports from developing countries in displacing jobs in import-competing industries is minor in comparison with other factors such as technological change and productivity growth." Indeed, protection against developing-country imports has sometimes accelerated the use of labor-saving equipment in the protected industry and thereby undermined the objective of preserving jobs.

Although the Northeast Asian countries have been apprehensive about growing protectionist trends, they realize that their economies depend preponderantly upon the health of the American and Japanese economies. For example, in 1978, Korea, Taiwan, and Hong Kong together drew upon the American market for 34 percent of their commodity exports and upon the Japanese market for 14 percent. A total of 5 percent went to Canada, Australia, and New Zealand combined. In turn, they absorbed 5 percent of America's exports, 13 percent of those from Japan, and 2 percent of those from the other developed countries of the region. In the last two decades, their growth has been largely supported by financial resources flowing from the United States and, to a lesser extent, Japan, and it has been facilitated by an inflow of technical skill and managerial know-how. Their economies will continue to grow only if this mechanism for international growth transmission is maintained.

For resource-poor countries, diversification of markets and products is the major recourse to take in maintaining export growth, especially when they are faced with the protectionism of industrialized countries. In fact, most managed to maintain a high export growth rate by this means in the years following the first oil crisis of 1973, an event which produced continuing economic stagnation in the industrial countries. Market diversification was reflected in the changes in the geographical distribution of exports from the Asia-Pacific countries during the 1970–1978 period. While all resource-rich countries in the region made gains in the percentage share of the Asia-Pacific market at the expense of countries from outside the region, all the region's resource-poor countries, including Japan, moved in the opposite direction by expanding markets in the Middle East, Africa, and South America. Korea is a good example. No other nation among the non-oil-producing developing countries channels so high a percentage (now approximately 10 percent) of her exports into the oil-producing world.

Trade policies adopted by the resource-scarce developing countries, no matter how different they may appear, have been largely dictated by the fact that their economies cannot survive without a continuing expansion of trade. These countries are increasingly aware that restrictive trade policies are not productive in the context of the complexities of current economic growth, and they know they must adapt their policies to the changing international economic environment. For example, Taiwan has been moving steadily toward liberalization of trade in recent years. Although her effort was slowed by balance-of-payment problems originating from the second oil crisis at the end of 1979, Korea has also been implementing an import-liberalization program since 1978. Her goal is to increase the scope of the automatic approval of imports from 50 percent where it stood in 1977 to 90 percent in 1982.

As regards Hong Kong and Singapore, there is no need to cite details since they are known throughout the world as typical free-trade areas. Located at economically strategic points in international trade, both maximize economic benefits from the free passage of merchandise through their ports and from the processing of raw materials imported from whatever source is most profitable. Singapore has a tariff system, but it is highly selective in scope and generally low in rate. Hong Kong, of course, has no tariff.

The ASEAN and Its Economic Potential

The five countries in Southeast Asia have been attracting increasing attention from other countries in the Asia-Pacific region because of their (1) great economic potential, (2) growing trade relations with other countries in the region, and (3) effort to establish common developmental and international affairs policies through the framework of ASEAN.

The ASEAN nations are middle-income, developing countries with per capita incomes that ranged between US$2,880 for Singapore and US$300 for Indonesia in 1977. The GNP of these countries equalled about 16 percent of that of Japan in 1978, and their combined exports amounted to less than 3 percent of the world's total exports during the same year.

In contrast to other countries in the region, during the 1970s the ASEAN countries achieved a higher rate of domestic output and export growth than in the 1960s, despite the fact it was a time of general economic setback throughout the world. This is due mainly to the buoyant, external demand for the region's primary resources and to the rapid growth of industrial production in Singapore.

The ASEAN countries possess an immense variety of natural resources (copper, tin, nickel, and petroleum among others) and primary agricultural commodities (especially palm oil, coconut oil, natural rubber, and timber). With a population of 250 million, more than twice that of Japan, the ASEAN region provides a growing market for both domestic output and foreign imports. The member nations are firmly committed to non-communist political goals and employ a free-enterprise system wherein public or state corporations also play a certain role.

Trade relations between ASEAN and other countries of the Asia-Pacific region expanded rapidly in the 1970s. In 1978, the combined exports of the member nations totaled over US$35 billion, of which US$25 billion, or 70 percent, was to countries in the Pacific region. For 1970, the figure was 63 percent. In the Asia-Pacific market, Japan and the United States are by far the most important customer countries, accounting for 25 and 20 percent of ASEAN's exports respectively. This compares with 24 and 17 percent for 1970 and shows that ASEAN's dependence on both countries for export markets has been increasing.

The importance of the three North Asian economies as a market for ASEAN goods has also been increasing. They accounted for 4 percent of total exports in 1970 and nearly 8 percent in 1978. ASEAN exports of course include trade among the member countries themselves. However, the proportion of intra-ASEAN trade has decreased steadily from 29 percent in 1970 to 20 percent in 1978, indicating that trade has become increasingly outward oriented. This is in contrast to ASEAN goals which center around the expansion of internal trade.

The ASEAN region presents an important market for countries in the Asia-Pacific region, although its significance varies from country to country. For Japan, the ASEAN countries are most important as a supply source for primary resources and as an export market. In 1977, for example, Japan depended on this region for 10 percent of her foodstuffs, 18 percent of her raw materials, and 15 percent of her mineral fuel (mostly from Indonesia). Disaggregation of this commodity group reveals an even more striking dependence—97 percent of her natural rubber, 99.6 percent of her tin and tin alloys, 42 percent of her wood, 37 percent of her copper ore concentrates, 74 percent of her nickel, 29 percent of her bauxites, and 23.7 percent of her sugar.

Japan is dominant in terms of foreign investments in the ASEAN nations. The growth of Japan's investment in the region has accelerated since 1972 when the Japanese government eliminated most restrictions on foreign investments. In fact, 80 percent of the accumulated current investment of US$4.5 billion was approved during the five years between 1972 and 1977. A major motivating factor for Japan's direct investment in the region is secured access to such basic resources as minerals, timber, petroleum, and agricultural resources. For this reason, Japanese investments thus far have been concentrated in resource-rich Indonesia which holds 68 percent of Japan's total investment in the region.

For the United States, ASEAN represents a smaller market than do the three semi-industrialized countries of Northeast Asia.

Unlike Japan, the United States does not depend heavily on the ASEAN market for primary resources, except for purchase of petroleum from Indonesia. In 1978 American exports to ASEAN totaled US$4.6 billion, or about 3 percent of the total. Still, this represents a fourfold increase over 1970 levels. Although small in absolute amounts, the American share in ASEAN's manufactured imports rose during the 1970s. While the United States trails Japan in direct investment—the total was estimated at some US$1 billion at the end of 1977, 80 percent of which is in Indonesia—it has been the major provider of bank capital. There are 124 American banks with US$17.3 billion in outstanding loans active in the ASEAN market. Such other industrialized countries as Canada and New Zealand have minor economic links with the ASEAN countries. Both exported less than US$200 million in goods during 1978. Australia, however, has strong links with Malaysia, Singapore, and Indonesia, where export levels reached US$1 billion in 1978.

The ASEAN economies provide a promising market to the newly industrializing countries in Northeast Asia. Between 1970 and 1978, combined exports of the three countries increased from US$400 million to US$2.8 billion, a sevenfold increase in an eight-year period. Partly because of their historical and cultural background and partly due to geographical vicinity, Hong Kong and Taiwan have closer links with the ASEAN countries than Korea. Each country has a trade volume exceeding US$1 billion, whereas Korea's trade totals less than US$500 million. For Hong Kong, the interport trade with Singapore is most important, while Korea and Taiwan are sending manufactured products in exchange for mineral and agricultural resources.

The Northeast Asian and ASEAN countries have been competing in international markets with respect to such labor-intensive products as textiles, clothing, plywood, and mechanical products, and the competition is expected to become keener in the future. With a level of technical and industrial sophistication currently ahead of ASEAN, the semi-industrialized countries are making efforts to supply the ASEAN market with such capital-intensive and skill-oriented products as machine tools, ships, rolling stock, communication equipment, and electronic products. Their success in this endeavor will largely depend upon the attitudes and commercial policies of ASEAN and the speed with which the group makes progress in its economic development.

Turning to the external policy of the ASEAN countries, it appears that the organization's major interest in international cooperation centers around the promotion of intraregional economic development within its own institutional framework. The Bangkok Declaration of 1967 indicates that the major objective of ASEAN is to accelerate economic growth in the region through joint endeavors, to collaborate more effectively with respect to agriculture and industry, and to expand trade with particular emphasis upon international commodity trade.

Since its inauguration, ASEAN has made important strides toward regional cooperation on a variety of fronts. One of the important achievements was an agreement called the Industrial Complementation Scheme, which was signed in February 1976. The scheme allocates investment projects among the member countries for specialized production and is protected by a special arrangement which includes guaranteed purchases and preferential tariffs. The economic logic behind the scheme is that it enables the ASEAN members to avoid the duplication of projects—"unnecessary competition"—and at the same time permits them to overcome the possible shortage of markets which could result from the production of the same products by the individual countries. At a meeting in 1976, Indonesia and Malaysia were each given a urea project, the Philippines a superphosphate project, Thailand a soda ash project, and Singapore a diesel engine project. The urea projects have started with the aid of soft loans provided by the Japanese government. In addition to these projects, there is another agreement on industrial complementation programs for investments which is restricted mainly to the private sector, but which operates under the guidelines provided by the governments. An agreement on rice stock programs has recently been completed as well.

However, the most significant achievement thus far is a Preferential Trading Agreement (PTA) which provides a mechanism for expanding regional trade through reduced trade barriers among the member countries. To date, exchanges in tariff concessions have been applied to 4,235 commodities, and the preferential list is expected to include more than 10,000 items by the end of 1980. To date, the effect of the PTA on regional trade has been rather modest, but it is a significant step toward the liberalization of trade within the region, and it may prove to be conducive to the future liberalization of trade beyond the boundaries of ASEAN proper.

It is often said that ASEAN is inward looking in its commercial policies as well as in its development strategy. However, this generalization overlooks the fact that Singapore, a free-trade nation, is a member of ASEAN. Moreover, there are noteworthy policy differences among the member countries, reflecting the resource position of individual countries. For example, Indonesia and Malaysia are more interested in a greater utilization of natural resources for industrializing their economies than the Philippines and Thailand. Recently a government leader from the Philippines stated that "today, the ASEAN economies are basically outward looking."

As previously noted, ASEAN trade with non-ASEAN countries has been increasing more rapidly than trade within the union. They now depend heavily on the extraregional market for the acquisition of manufactured products which in turn comprise more than half of their imports. They are pushing import-substituting types of industrialization forward, but they still need complementary resources for both project construction and project operation purposes which are obtainable only from foreign sources. In this regard, one authority has stated that because of ASEAN's emphasis on import-substituting industrialization, total imports of capital and producer goods have grown more rapidly than total exports. These facts strongly suggest that the ASEAN member countries should stand to benefit from a reduction of trade barriers both within and without the organization.

Conclusion

This discussion began with a search for the major factors responsible for current interest in forming a Pacific community. The foregoing analysis suggests several key factors:

1. *The Relative Decline of the American Position in the World Economy.* The leadership role of the United States in maintaining a free and open system of international trade weakened

during the 1970s in conjunction with the nation's relative decline as a world economic power. The United States now finds itself in need of a framework within which the recent changes can be more effectively managed and the strategic economic and security concerns of its foreign policy more effectively promoted.

2. *The Rise of Japan's Position in the Asia-Pacific and World Economy.* The phenomenal expansion of the Japanese economy in the post–World War II period has placed the nation in a unique position wherein she needs closer economic relations with other Asian economies in order to secure a supply of natural resources and maintain a market for her exports. Both needs are essential to her survival. As a corollary, Japan has to play a leadership role in Asia if she is—as she must—to harmonize her interests with those of the other countries of the region.

3. *The Increasing Role of the Resource-Rich Countries.* Canada, Australia, and New Zealand, countries traditionally tied to the Atlantic economies, now see their future more in Asia-Pacific terms than Atlantic terms. The resource-rich developing countries in Southeast Asia have gained in economic importance since the energy crisis of 1973 and are now attracting considerable attention throughout the Asia-Pacific region.

4. *The Emergence of Newly Industrializing Countries.* The small economies of Northeast Asia, in conjunction with Singapore to the south, are attracting growing attention from all quarters. They have led most of the world in terms of dynamic economic growth since the middle 1960s. In a sense peripheral to the Asia-Pacific arena as regards natural resources and international influence, these nations are by necessity interested in freer access to all international markets, within the limits of political feasibility. Thus, regional or international economic cooperation is of great importance to them.

These factors point to a growing and complex interdependence among the countries of the Asia-Pacific region. This interdependence inevitably involves conflicting as well as common interests which will work to shape the course of future events. The question is whether this course will be guided by the whim of self-interest or a concerted effort to harmonize conflicting interests and promote the common good. A comparison of the economic experience of the 1960s with that of the 1970s clearly indicates that the manner and degree of international cooperation makes a marked difference in the speed with which countries can progress toward their goal of economic advancement.

International trade lies at the center of international economic development, and therefore trade policies occupy a central position with respect to international economic cooperation. There must be concern over the recent worldwide drift toward protectionism. A pessimistic view suggests that a liberal trade regime is a thing of the past. Our study, however, suggests that there are also forces at work on behalf of freer trade. The United States, with its low dependence on trade, could choose to become a self-reliant global power. It is unlikely, however, that it will abandon its responsibility to help preserve a liberal and open system of international commerce, something that lies at the very foundation of its commitment to a free and prosperous world. The self-restraint it has shown recently in dealing with the influx of Japanese automobiles, a matter with far-reaching consequences for its own auto industry, strongly suggests this conclusion.

Japan's interest in freer trade is likewise real because of her particular economic circumstances. The resource-scarce developing economies of Northeast Asia and Singapore are in a similar position. Their support for freer trade is also dictated by the basic nature of their economies. The ASEAN powers present a somewhat different case, but their move toward freer trade within their own institutional structure is testimony that they acknowledge the benefits that accrue from a liberal trade policy.

All of this leads to the final conclusion that freer trade policies, no matter how desirable, require leadership from the major market powers of the area—the United States and Japan. The interests of both will be served by such policies and both can anticipate mutual support as well as support from the developing and newly developed countries in this effort. This, of course, is the strongest argument possible for greater regional cooperation and the formation of a Pacific community. Regrettably, all have tended to shy away from addressing this argument directly. But whether or not they reverse course and pick up the mantle of leadership, the fact remains that trade policy still lies at the heart of international cooperation.

APPENDIX A
Pacific Basin Regional Organizations

The following listing is the first known attempt to compile a roster of the international organizations active in the Pacific Basin. In an effort to maintain reasonable limits, it cites only those groups with a primary concern for the region, an applied purpose, and a multilateral focus. It does not list such organizations as the various United Nations agencies (except those functioning primarily within the region), the innumerable Asian and Pacific academic programs, and the many bilateral consultative groups. Further information on most organizations cited may be found in the *Yearbook of International Organizations* and similar publications.

Afro-Asian Housing Organization (AAHO), P.O. Box 523, Cairo, Egypt.

Afro-Asian Institute for Co-operative and Labour Studies, P.O. Box 16201, Tel Aviv, Israel.

Afro-Asian Organisation for Economic Co-operation (AFRASEC), c/o Cairo Chamber of Commerce Building, Midan-Al-Fataki, Bab El Louk, Cairo, Egypt.

Afro-Asian Paediatric Association, Jinnah Postgraduate Medical Center, Karachi 4, Pakistan.

Afro-Asian Peoples' Solidarity Organization (AAPSO), 89 Abdel Aziz Al Saoud Street, Manial, Cairo, Egypt.

Afro-Asian Rural Reconstruction Organization (AARRO), 117–118 Defence Colony, New Delhi 110024, India.

Afro-Asian Writers' Permanent Bureau, 104 Kasr El-Aini Street, Cairo, Egypt.

Agricultural Development Council (Asia) (ADC), 1290 Avenue of the Americas, New York, NY 10019, U.S.A.

The American-ASEAN Trade Council, Inc. (AATC), 501 Madison Avenue, New York, NY 10022, U.S.A.

American-Asian Educational Exchange, 88 Morningside Drive, New York, NY 10027, U.S.A.

ASEAN Business Council, SGV Building, 6760 Ayala Avenue, Makati, Metro Manila, Philippines.

ASEAN Chambers of Commerce and Industry (ASEAN CCI), Chinese Chamber of Commerce Building #201, Hill Street, Singapore 0617, Singapore.

ASEAN–U.S. Business Council, ASEAN Section, P.O. Box 631 MCC, Makati, Metro Manila, Philippines; U.S. Section, Chamber of Commerce of the United States, 1615 H Street, N.W., Washington, D.C. 20006, U.S.A.

Asia Foundation, P.O. Box 3223, San Francisco, CA 94119, U.S.A.

Asia-Pacific Academy of Ophthalmology, 1013 Bishop Street # 280, Honolulu, HI 96813, U.S.A.

Asia-Pacific Council of American Chambers of Commerce (APCAC), 701 Toshio Building, 2-2 Marunouchi 3-chome, Chiyoda-ku, Tokyo 100, Japan.

Asia-Pacific Forestry Commission, c/o FAO Regional Office, Maliwan Mansion, Phra Atit Road, Bangkok, Thailand.

Asia-Pacific Printers Federation, 16-8, 1-chome, Shintomi, Chuo-ku, Tokyo, Japan.

Asia-Pacific Socialist Organization (APSO), Wellington, New Zealand.

Asia-Pacific Telecommunity, c/o ESCAP, United Nations Building, Rajadamnern Avenue, Bangkok 2, Thailand.

Asia Society, 112 East 64th Street, New York, NY 10021, U.S.A.

Asian-African Legal Consultative Committee, 20 Ring Road, Lajpat Nagar-IV, New Delhi 110024, India.

Asian Amateur Athletic Association (AAAA), Rabaria Mohalla, Ajmer, India.

Asian Area Aquatic Environment Research and Training Institute, c/o

Chubu Economic Federation (Chukeiren), 1-1 Shinsakae-machi, Naka-ku, Nagoya 460, Japan.

Asian Association for Biology Education (AABE), Mahaweli Maha Vidyalaya, Vasanakande, Katugastota, Sri Lanka.

Asian Association of Development Research and Training Institutes, P.O. Box 2-136, Sri Ayudhya Road, Bangkok, Thailand.

Asian Association of Gastroenterology, P.O. Box 2598, Manila, Philippines.

Asian Association of Pediatric Surgeons (AAPS), c/o Department of Pediatric Surgery, Juntendo University School of Medicine, 3 Hongo, Bunkyo-ku, Tokyo 113, Japan.

Asian Association of Personnel Management (AAPM), c/o Bengal Chamber of Commerce and Industry, 23 AN Mookerjee Road, Calcutta 700001, India.

Asian and Australasian Hotel and Restaurant Association (AAHRA), 206 Koalim Building, Kramat Lane, Singapore 9, Singapore.

Asian Badminton Confederation (ABC), 35 Jalan Tempinis Satu, Bungsar Lucky Gardens, Kuala Lumpur 22-04, Malaysia.

Asian Baptist Fellowship (ABF), 11-54 Shirley Road, Wollstonecraft, NSW 2065, Australia.

Asian Basketball Confederation (ABC), IPO Box 1106, Seoul, Korea.

Asian Benevolent Corps (ABC), 2142 F Street, NW, Washington, D.C. 20037, U.S.A.

Asian Billiards Confederation (ABC), Toshimaen Amusement Park, 3-25-1 Kooyama, Nerimaku, Tokyo, Japan.

Asian Broadcasting Union (ABU), c/o NHK Broadcasting Centre, 2-2-1 Jinnan, Shibuya-ku, Tokyo 150, Japan.

Asian Buddhist Conference for Peace (ABCP), 8-7 Shinsen-cho, Shibuya-ku, Tokyo, Japan.

Asian Buddhist Peace Association, 214-2 Higashi-Saurizuka, Chiba-ken, Japan.

Asian Center of Educational Innovation for Development (ACEID), P.O. Box 1425, Bangkok, Thailand.

Asian Centre for Comparative Education (ACCET), University of Azarabadgan, Tabriz, Iran.

Asian Centre for Development Administration (ACDA), 3 Jalan Spooner, Lake Gardens, Kuala Lumpur 01-02, Malaysia.

Asian Centre for Training and Research in Social Welfare and Development, Makati, Metro Manila, Philippines.

Asian Christian Peace Conference (ACPC), United Theological College, 17 Miller's Road, Bangalore 560046, India.

Asian Clearing Union, c/o Bank Markazi Iran, Ferdowsi Avenue, Teheran, Iran.

Asian Club, World Trade Center Building #706, 2-4-1 Hamamatsucho, Minato-ku, Tokyo 105, Japan.

Asian Committee for People's Organization (ACPO), 509 Padre Faura Street, Ermita D-406, Manila, Philippines.

Asian Committee for Standardization of Physical Fitness Tests (ACSPFT), c/o Laboratory of Physical Fitness, Tokyo Metropolitan University, 1-1-1 Yagumo, Meguro-ku, Tokyo, Japan.

Asian Confederation of Credit Unions (ACCU), c/o Korea Credit Union League Suhdaemoon, P.O. Box 8, Seoul, Korea.

Asian Conservation Laboratory, P.O. Drawer F, Mohawk, NY 13407, U.S.A.

Asian Cultural Exchange Foundation, c/o Joan M. Briskin, Development Office, Towson State University, Towson, MD 21204, U.S.A.

Asian Cultural Forum on Development (ACFOD), Siri Building #201, 399/1 Soi Siri, Off Silom Road, Bangkok 5, Thailand.

Asian Development Bank (ADB), 2330 Roxas Boulevard, Pasay City, P.O. Box 789, Manila, Philippines.

Asian Development Center (ADC), Philbanking Corporation Building, Anda Circle, Port Area, Manila, Philippines.

Asian Development Fund, c/o Asian Development Bank, 2330 Roxas Boulevard, Pasay City, P.O. Box 789, Manila, Philippines.

Asian Environmental Council, 1787-9 Petchburi Gallery Building, New Petchburi Road, Bangkok, Thailand.

Asian Environmental Society (AES), 36 Redwood Street, Fairview, Quezon City, Philippines.

Asian Federation of UNESCO Clubs and Associations (AFUCA), Asahi-

Seimei Building, 6-1 Marunouchi 1-chome, Chiyoda-ku, Tokyo 100, Japan.

Asian Football Confederation (AFC), 88 Jalan Sultan Idris Shah, Ipoh, Malaysia.

Asian Games Federation (AGF), Kakhe-Varzesh, Teheran, Iran.

Asian Hemophiliacs Rescue Association, Green Cross Corporation, 1-3 Gamau-Cho-Joto-ku, Osaka, Japan.

Asian Highway Co-ordinating Committee, c/o ESCAP, United Nations Building, Rajadamnern Avenue, Bangkok 2, Thailand.

Asian Institute for Economic Development and Planning, P.O. Box 2136, Sri Ayudhya Road, Bangkok, Thailand.

Asian Institute of Educational Planning and Administration, Indraprastha Estate, Ring Road, New Delhi 1, India.

Asian Institute of Technology, P.O. Box 2754, Rangsit, Bangkok, Thailand.

Asian Judo Union, c/o Kodokan Judo Institute, 16630 1-chome, Kasuga, Bunkyo-ku, Tokyo, Japan.

Asian Mass Communication Research and Information Centre (AMIC), 39 Newton Road, Singapore 11, Singapore.

Asian Network for Industrial Technology Information and Extension (TECHNONET), RELC International House, 30 Orange Grove Road, Tanglin, P.O. Box 160, Singapore 10, Singapore.

Asian and Oceanian Association of Neurology, c/o Division of Neurology, Ramathibodi Hospital, Rama 6 Road, Bangkok, Thailand.

Asian-Oceanic Postal Union (AOPU), Post Office Building, Manila 2801, Philippines.

Asian and Pacific Centre for Women and Development, c/o UNDP Office, United Nations Building, P.O. Box 1555, Teheran, Iran.

Asian and Pacific Coconut Community (APCC), Pantja Niaga Building, 94-96 Kramat Raya, P.O. Box 343, Jakarta, Indonesia.

Asian and Pacific Cultural Association (ASPACA), KPO Box 196, Seoul, Korea.

Asian Pacific Dental Federation (APDF), c/o Dr. Robert Y. Norton, 183 Macquarie Street, Sydney, NSW 2000, Australia.

Asian Pacific Dental Student Association (APDSA), c/o Japan Dental Association, Kita 4-6-20 Kudan, Chiyoda-ku, Tokyo, Japan.

Asian Pacific League of Physical Medicine and Rehabilitation, c/o Department of Physical Medicine and Rehabilitation, Jinnah Postgraduate Medical Centre, Karachi-35, Pakistan.

Asian Pacific Paediatric Gastro-enterology Group, c/o Medical School, University of Indonesia, Jalan Salemba 6, Jakarta, Indonesia.

Asian Pacific Section of the International Confederation of Plastic and Reconstructive Surgery, c/o Prof. R. L. Manchanda, Misri Bazar, Patiala, Punjab, India.

Asian-Pacific Society of Cardiology (APSC), c/o Hawaii Heart Association, 245 N. Kukui Street, Honolulu, HI 96817, U.S.A.

Asian-Pacific Weed Science Society (APWSS), c/o Department of Agronomy and Soil Science, University of Hawaii at Manoa, 3190 Maile Way, Honolulu, HI 96822, U.S.A.

Asian Packaging Federation (APF), Far East Building #405, MCC P.O. Box 1058, Makati, Rizal 3117, Philippines.

Asian Packaging Information Centre (APIC), Eldex Building #21, A Ma Tau Wei Road, Hunghom, Kowloon, Hong Kong.

Asian Parasite Control Organization (APCO), c/o Hoken Kaikan Bekkan, 1-2 Sadohara-cho, Ichigaya, Shinjuku-ku, Tokyo 162, Japan.

Asian Parliamentarians Union (APU), Room 604, 10-2, 2-chome, Nagata-cho, Chiyoda-ku, Tokyo, Japan.

Asian Patent Attorneys Association (APAA), c/o Kyowa Patent and Law Office, Fuji Building, 2-3, Marunouchi 3-chome, Chiyoda-ku, Tokyo 100, Japan.

Asian Productivity Organization (APO), Aoyama Dai-Ichi Mansions, 4-14, Akasaka 8-chome, Minato-ku, Tokyo 107, Japan.

Asian Programme of Educational Innovation for Development (APEID), c/o ACEID, 920 Sukhumvit Road, CPO Box 1425, Bangkok, Thailand.

Asian Regional Communication Network (ARICN), c/o Agricultural Development Council, 1290 Avenue of the Americas, New York, NY 10017, U.S.A.

Asian Regional Institute for School Building Research, UNDP Representative, P.O. Box 1505, Colombo 7, Sri Lanka.

Pacific Basin Regional Organizations 145

Asian Regional Medical Student Association (ARMSA), c/o Faculty of Medicine, University of Malaya, Kuala Lumpur, Malaysia.

Asian Secretaries Association, c/o SAPES, P.O. Box 411, Colombo Court Post Office, Singapore 6, Singapore.

Asian Society for Comparative Education (ASCE), c/o Dr. J. C. Sharma, University of Azarabadgan, Tabriz, Iran.

Asian South Pacific Bureau of Adult Education (ASPBAE), Indian Adult Education Association, 17B Indraprastha Marg, New Delhi 110001, India.

Asian Statistical Institute (ASI), Economic Cooperation Centre Building Annex, P.O. Box 13, Akasaka, Tokyo 107, Japan.

Asian Students Association (ASA), c/o HKFS, 511 Nathan Road, 1/F, Kowloon, Hong Kong.

Asian Student's Cultural Association, 12-13 Honkamagome 2-chome, Bunkyo-ku, Tokyo 113, Japan.

Asian Vegetable Research and Development Center (AVRDC), P.O. Box 42, Shanhua, Tainan 741, Taiwan.

Asian Weightlifting Federation (AWF), Sports Feds Joint Bureau, P.O. Box 11-1642, Teheran, Iran.

Asian Women's Institute, c/o Dr. Eva I. Shipstone, Isabella Thoburn College, Lucknow, India.

Asian Youth Council, c/o National Youth Leadership Training Institute, South Bouna Vista Road, Singapore, Singapore.

Association of Asian-American Chambers of Commerce (AAACC), P.O. Box 2801, Washington, D.C. 20013, U.S.A.

Association of Asian Social Science Research Councils (AASSREC), c/o Indian Council of Social Science Research, IIPA Hostel Building, Indraprastha Estate, New Delhi 110001, India.

Association of Christian Institutions for Social Concern in Asia, ESII, Bidhan Nagar, Durgapur 12, WB, India.

Association Europe-Japan, 48 rue de la Fayette, F-75009 Paris, France.

Association of Natural Rubber Producing Countries (ANRPC), Bangunan Getah Asli, 150 Jalan Ampang, Kuala Lumpur, Malaysia.

Association of Pediatric Societies of the Southeast Asian Region (APS-

SEAR), Medical Center Manila #306, 1122 General Luna Street, Ermita, P.O. Box EA 100, Manila, Philippines.

Association for Science Cooperation in Asia (ASCA), address unavailable.

Association of South East Asian Nations (ASEAN), c/o Department of Foreign Affairs, Jalan Taman Pejambon 6, Jakarta, Indonesia.

Association of South East Asian Publishers (ASEAP), c/o University of Malaysia Press, Pantai Valley, Kuala Lumpur, Malaysia.

Association of Southeast Asian Institutions of Higher Learning (ASAIHL), c/o Chulalongkorn University, Henri Dunant Road, Bangkok 5, Thailand.

Association of Surgeons of South-East Asia, c/o Prof. G. B. Ong, University of Hong Kong, Hong Kong.

ANZUS Council, Department of External Affairs, Canberra, ACT 2600, Australia.

Brotherhood of Asian Trade Unionists (BATU), Vermont Towers #2F, Julio Nakpil Street, Malate, P.O. Box 163, Manila, Philippines.

Centre for the Development of Human Resources in Rural Asia (CENDHRRA), P.O. Box 458, Greenhills, San Juan, Rizal 3113, Philippines.

Christian Conference of Asia (CCA), c/o Rev. Dr. Yap Kim Hao, 480 Lorong 2, Toa Payoh, Singapore 12, Singapore.

Colombo Plan for Cooperative Economic Development in South and South-East Asia, Colombo Plan Bureau, BP Box 596, Colombo, Sri Lanka.

Commission of Asian and Pacific Affairs of the International Chamber of Commerce (ICC-CAPA), 150 Rajbopit Road, Bangkok 2, Thailand.

Committee for Coordination of Investigations of the Lower Mekong Basin, c/o ESCAP, Sala Santitham, Bangkok 2, Thailand.

Committee for Co-ordination of Joint Prospecting for Mineral Resources in Asian Offshore Areas and in the South Pacific (CCOP), UNDP/CCOP, United Nations Building, Rajadamnern Avenue, Bangkok 2, Thailand.

Confederation of ASEAN Journalists, Persatuan Wartawan Indonesia, Jalan Veteran 7-C, Jakarta, Indonesia.

Confederation of Asian Chambers of Commerce and Industry (CACCI),

Chambers of Commerce of the Philippines Building, Magallanes Drive, Manila, Philippines.

Conference of Southeast Asian Librarians (CONSAL), c/o Rubber Research Institute of Malaysia-Library, P.O. Box 150, Kuala Lumpur, Malaysia.

Coordinating Committee of South-East Asian Senior Officials on Transport and Communications (COORDCOM), c/o Ministry of Transport, Kuala Lumpur, Malaysia.

Council for Asian Manpower Studies (CAMS), P.O. Box 127, Quezon City, Philippines.

Council of Ministers for Asian Economic Cooperation, c/o ESCAP, United Nations Building, Rajadamnern Avenue, Bangkok 2, Thailand.

East Asia Travel Association, c/o Japan National Tourist Organization, 2-10-1, Yurakucho, Chiyoda-ku, Tokyo, Japan.

East-West Center, 1777 East-West Road, Honolulu, HI 96848, U.S.A.

Eastern Regional Organization for Planning and Housing (EAROPH), 4-A Ring Road, Indraprastha Estate, New Delhi 110002, India.

Eastern Regional Organization for Public Administration (EROPA), Rizal Hall, Padre Faura Street, P.O. Box 474, Manila, Philippines.

Economic Cooperation Centre for the Asian and Pacific Region (ECOCEN), c/o National Economic Development Board, Ministry of Economy, Rajadamnoen Klang, Bangkok, Thailand.

Far East-America Council of Commerce and Industry, 1270 Avenue of the Americas, New York, NY 10020, U.S.A.

Far East Conference (FEC), 11 Broadway, New York, NY 10004, U.S.A.

Far East Merchants Association (FEMAS), 5432 152nd Street, Flushing, NY 11355, U.S.A.

Federation of Afro-Asian Insurers and Reinsurers (FAIR), address unavailable.

Federation of ASEAN Shippers Council (FASC), c/o Department of Foreign Affairs, Jalan Taman Pejambon 6, Jakarta, Indonesia.

Federation of Asian Bishops Conferences (FABC), P.O. Box 3819, Malate, Manila, Philippines.

Federation of Asian Nutrition Societies (FANS), Nutrition Foundation of the Philippines, 107 East Rodriguez Boulevard, Quezon City D-502, Philippines.

Federation of Asian and Oceanian Biochemists (FAOB), c/o Department of Biochemistry, Victoria University of Wellington, Wellington, New Zealand.

Federation of Asian Pharmaceutical Associations (FAPA), Hizon Building, 29 Quezon Boulevard, Quezon City, Philippines.

Federation of Asian Women's Associations (FAWA), NFWC Building, 962 Josefa Llanes Escoda Street, Ermita, Manila, Philippines.

Federation of Endocrine Societies of Asia and Oceania, c/o Department of Medicine, Sydney Hospital, Sydney, NSW 2000, Australia.

Food and Agriculture Organization of the United Nations (FAO): Asia and the Far East, Maliwan Mansion, Phra Atit Road, Bangkok 2, Thailand.

Foundation for the Peoples of the South Pacific (FSP), P.O. Box 3395, Sydney, NSW 2001, Australia.

Free Pacific Association, 86 Riverside Drive, New York, NY 10024, U.S.A.

Group of Caribbean and Pacific States (ACP Group), 451 Avenue George Henri, B-1200 Brussels, Belgium.

Hawaii International Services Agency, 130 Merchant Street #130, Honolulu, HI 96813, U.S.A.

Hawaii World Trade Association, 1735 Bishop Street #220, Honolulu, HI 96813, U.S.A.

Henry Luce Foundation, 111 West 50th Street, New York, NY 10020, U.S.A.

Indo-Pacific Fisheries Council (IPFC), c/o FAO Regional Office, Maliwan Mansion, Phra Atit Road, Bangkok 2, Thailand.

Institute for the Development of Agricultural Cooperation in Asia (IDACA), 24-9, 6-chome, Funabashi, Setagayaku, Tokyo, Japan.

Institute of Economic Growth: Research Center on Social and Economic Development in Asia, University Enclave, Delhi 7, India.

Inter-American Tropical Tuna Commission (IATTC), c/o Scripps Institution of Oceanography, La Jolla, CA 92037, U.S.A.

International Association of Orientalist Librarians, c/o Graduate School of Library Studies, University of Hawaii at Manoa, 2425 Campus Road, Honolulu, HI 96822, U.S.A.

International Confederation of Free Trade Unions: Asian Regional Organization (ICFTU:ARO), P-20 Green Park Extension, New Delhi 110016, India.

International Co-operative Alliance: Regional Office and Education Centre for South-East Asia, 43 Friends Colony (East), New Delhi 110014, India.

International Crops Research Institute for the Semi-Arid Tropics (ICRISAT), 1-11-256 Begumpet, Hyderabad, India.

International Federation of Asian and Western Pacific Contractors' Association (IFAWPCA), Makati Commercial Center, Metro Manila, P.O. Box 1664, Makati, Philippines.

International Institute for Economic Development, c/o International Islamic Organization, J 1 Let Jen S Parman No. 66, Slipi Raya, Jakarta, Indonesia.

International North Pacific Fisheries Commission (NPFC), 6640 Northwest Marine Drive, Vancouver, B.C., Canada.

International Planned Parenthood Federation: East and South-East Asia and Oceania Region, 246 Jalan Ampang, Kuala Lumpur 16-03, Malaysia.

International Rice Commission, c/o FAO Regional Office, Maliwan Mansion, Phra Atit Road, Bangkok 2, Thailand.

International Rice Research Institute (IRRI), P.O. Box 933, Manila, Philippines.

International Society of Hematology: Asian-Pacific Division, Apartado Postal 41-711, Mexico 10, DF Mexico.

International Tsunami Information Center (ITIC), P.O. Box 3830, Honolulu, HI 96812, U.S.A.

International Union for Oriental and Asian Studies, 77 quai du Port-au-Fouarre, F-94199 Saint-Maur, France.

Korean Cultural and Freedom Foundation (Asia) (KCFF), 1800 Briarwood Ridge Road, McLean, VA 22101, U.S.A.

Latin American Regional Association of Pacific Ports, c/o Empresa Portuaria de Chile, Casilla No 133-V, Valparaiso, Chile.

Law Association for Asia and the Western Pacific (LAWASIA), c/o Faculty of Law, University of New South Wales, Kensington, NSW 2033, Australia.

Near East Foundation, 54 East 64th Street, New York, NY 10017, U.S.A.

North Pacific Fur Seal Commission (NPFSC), c/o National Marine Fisheries Service, Washington, D.C. 20235, U.S.A.

Obor Foundation for Cultural and Intellectual Exchange between Southeast Asia and the West, 623 Greenhill Road, Madison, CT 06443, U.S.A.

Oceania Football Confederation, 111 Apirana Avenue, P.O. Box 029, Glen Innes, Auckland 6, New Zealand.

Oceania Judo Union (OJU), 52 Fordham Road, Hawthorn, VIC 3122, Australia.

Organization of Afro-Asian Latin American Peoples Solidarity, Apartado 4224, Havana, Cuba.

Organization of Asian News Agencies (OANA), Antara News Agency, 53 Jalan Antara, P.O. Box 257, Jakarta, Indonesia.

Orient Airlines Association (OAA), SBTC Building #1103, Ayala Avenue, Makati, Philippines.

Oriental Missionary Society (OMS), P.O. Box A, Greenwood, IN 46142, U.S.A.

Oriental Numismatic Society (ONS), 30 Warren Road, Woodley, Reading, Berkshire, UK.

Pacific Area Standards Congress (PASC), c/o American National Standards Institute, 1430 Broadway, New York, NY 10018, U.S.A.

Pacific Area Travel Association (PATA), 228 Grant Avenue, San Francisco, CA 94108, U.S.A.

Pacific-Asia Resources Center (PARC), P.O. Box 5250, Tokyo, Japan.

Pacific-Asian Conference of Municipalities (PACOM), c/o Managing Director's Office, City and County of Honolulu, Honolulu, HI 96813, U.S.A.

Pacific Asian Federation of Industrial Engineering (PAFIE), B-37, Greater Kailash, New Delhi 48, India.

Pacific Basin Center Foundation, address unavailable.

Pacific Basin Development Council, 567 South King Street #620, Honolulu, HI 96813, U.S.A.

Pacific Basin Economic Council (PBEC), c/o Associated Chambers of Manufacturers of Australia, Industry House, Barton, ACT 2600, Australia.

Pacific Conference of Churches, P.O. Box 2401, Suva, Fiji.

Pacific Council of Japan, c/o Prof. Ato Matsuda, Waseda University, Tokyo 160, Japan.

Pacific Forum, 190 South King Street #1376, Honolulu, HI 96813, U.S.A.

Pacific Industrial Property Association (PIPA), 277 Park Avenue #1000, New York, NY 10017, U.S.A.

Pacific International Trapshooting Association (PITA), 3847 Glenwood Loop SE, Salem, OR 97301, U.S.A.

Pacific Islands News Association, c/o Extension Services, University of the South Pacific, Suva, Fiji.

Pacific Islands Producers Association, P.O. Box 1224, Suva, Fiji.

Pacific Science Association (PSA), c/o Bernice P. Bishop Museum, P.O. Box 17801, Honolulu, HI 96817, U.S.A.

Pacific Scientific Research Institute of Fisheries and Oceanography (TINRO), UL Leninskaya 20, Vladivostok, U.S.S.R.

Pacific Telecommunications Council, 1110 University Avenue #303, Honolulu, HI 96826, U.S.A.

Pacific Trade and Development Conferences (PAFTAD), c/o Professor Peter Drysdale, The Australian National University, P.O. Box 4, Canberra, ACT 2600, Australia.

Pacific Women's Resource Centre, YWCA Centre, Sukuna Park, Box 534, Suva, Fiji.

The Pan Pacific Community Association, 2011 I Street NW, Washington, D.C. 20006, U.S.A.

Pan Pacific Public Relations Federation (PPPRF), P.O. Box 4034, Honolulu, HI 96813, U.S.A.

Pan Pacific and Southeast Asia Women's Association (PPSEAWA), 9407 109th Drive, Sun City, AZ 85351, U.S.A.

Pan-Pacific Surgical Association, 1013 Bishop Street #236, Honolulu, HI 96813, U.S.A.

Permanent Commission for the South Pacific, Casilla 16199, Correo 9, Santiago, Chile.

Plant Protection Committee for the South East Asia and Pacific Region, c/o FAO Regional Office, Maliwan Mansion, Phra Atit Road, Bangkok 2, Thailand.

Press Foundation of Asia (PFA), Magsaysay Center Building, Roxas Boulevard, Manila, Philippines.

Regional Centre for Energy, Heat and Mass Transfer for Asia and Pacific, c/o Department of Science and Technology, New Delhi, India.

Regional Institute of Higher Education and Development (RIHED), CSSDI Building, Heng Mui Keng Terrace, Off 6 3/4 ms Pasir Panjang Road, Singapore 5, Singapore.

Seismological Society of the South-West Pacific (SSSWP), c/o Seismological Observatory, P.O. Box 1320, Wellington, New Zealand.

Society for the Advancement of Breeding Researches in Asia and Oceania (SABRAO), c/o Biology Department, National University of Malaysia, Kuala Lumpur, Malaysia.

Society for Asian and Comparative Philosophy, 1993 East-West Road, Honolulu, HI 96822, U.S.A.

South Asian Regional Branch of the International Council on Archives (SARBICA), c/o National Archives of Malaysia, Petaling Jaya, Malaysia.

South and East Asia Area Committee of the World Alliance of YMCAs, c/o YMCA Institute in Hong Kong, 23 Waterloo Road, Kowloon, Hong Kong.

South East Asia Association for the Promotion of Church Music, c/o Dr. Heywood Wong, 57 Peking Road, Kowloon, Hong Kong.

South East Asia Centre for the Promotion of Trade, Investments and Tourism (SEAPCENTRE), Kyodotshushin-kaikan, 2 Aoicho, Akasaka, Minato-ku, Tokyo, Japan.

South East Asia Iron and Steel Institute (SEAISI), Tower 1003, DBS Building, 6 Shenton Way, Singapore 1, Singapore.

South-East Asia Lumber Producers Association (SEALPA), address unavailable.

South East Asia and Pacific League against Rheumatism (SEAPAL), c/o Department of Medicine, Royal Melbourne Hospital, Melbourne, VIC 3050, Australia.

South East Asian Social Science Association, c/o Faculty of Political Science, Chulalongkorn University, Bangkok, Thailand.

Southeast Asia Press Centre, Kuala Lumpur, Malaysia.

Southeast Asia Regional Council for Adult Education, c/o Adult and Community Educators National Organization, Bureau of Public Schools, Arroceros Street, Manila, Philippines.

Southeast Asia Treaty Organization (SEATO) Cholera Research Laboratory, Dacca, Bangladesh.

Southeast Asia Treaty Organization (SEATO) Clinical Research Laboratory, Bangkok, Thailand.

Southeast Asia Treaty Organization (SEATO) Medical Research Laboratory, Bangkok, Thailand.

Southeast Asian Fisheries Development Center, Changi, Singapore 17, Singapore.

Southeast Asian Ministers of Education Organization (SEAMEO), Darakarn Building, 920 Sukhumwit Road, Bangkok 11, Thailand.

Southeast Asian Society of Soil Engineering (SEASSE), c/o Asian Institute of Technology, P.O. Box 2754, Rangsit, Bangkok, Thailand.

South Pacific Air Transport Council (SPATC), c/o Department of Civil Aviation, Melbourne, Victoria 3000, Australia.

South Pacific Appropriate Technology Foundation (SPATF), P.O. Box 6937, Boroko, Papua New Guinea.

South Pacific Bureau for Economic Cooperation (SPEC), GPO Box 856, Suva, Fiji.

South Pacific Commission (SPC), BP D5, Noumea, New Caledonia.

South Pacific Dental Secretariat, c/o Dental Division, Motootua Hospital, Apia Western Samoa.

South Pacific Forum, c/o SPEC, GPO 856, Suva, Fiji.

South Pacific Islands Fisheries Development Agency (SPIFDA), c/o South Pacific Commission, BP D5, Noumea, New Caledonia.

South Pacific Social Sciences Association, Box 5083, Suva, Fiji.

Southern Cross International (SCI), 79 Church Road, London NW4, UK.

Statistical Institute for Asia and the Pacific, Economic Cooperation Centre Building Annex, 42 Honmura-cho, Ichigaya Shinjuku-ku, Tokyo 162, Japan.

Student Travel Association of Asia (STAA), Manila, Philippines.

Textile Workers' Asian Regional Organization (TWARO), Zensen Kaikan Building, 8-16 Kudan Minami 4-chome, Chiyoda-ku, Tokyo, Japan.

United Nations Asian and Pacific Development Institute, United Nations Building, Rajadamnern Avenue, Bangkok 2, Thailand.

United Nations Economic and Social Commission for Asia and the Pacific (ESCAP), United Nations Building, Rajadamnern Avenue, Bangkok 2, Thailand.

U.S. Council for Southeast Asian Trade and Investment (SEATI), 1729 East Palm Canyon Drive, Palm Springs, CA 92262, U.S.A.

Volunteers in Asia (VIA), Box 4543, Stanford, CA 94305, U.S.A.

Western Pacific Orthopaedic Association (WPOA), 6 Illinois Street Cubao, Quezon City, Philippines.

APPENDIX B
The Organization for Pacific Trade and Development Proposal

The action portion of the Patrick-Drysdale study (pp. 18-25) is reprinted in full below. With the exception of certain footnotes, abbreviated in the actual report and here expanded to full form, it appears as in the original document.

1. History and Evolution of the OPTAD Concept

The advocacy of an Organization for Pacific Trade and Development [OPTAD] grew out of the debate over the desirability of a Pacific Free Trade Area.[1] The idea of a formal Pacific association was first espoused by the Japanese at an official level when in 1967 the then Foreign Minister, Takeo Miki, outlined his ideas for an "Asian Pacific policy" based on an "awareness of common principles," regional cooperation in Asia, cooperation among the advanced nations in the Pacific area and more extensive aid programs. Although there were no major policy initiatives while Miki was Foreign Minister, the Pacific Trade and Development Conference (PAFTAD Conference) series was launched, with Japanese Foreign Ministry support, to consider the Pacific Free Trade Area proposal. This conference series has involved policy-oriented academic economists, many of whom have served as advisers to their governments, plus some government officials in their private capacity, who are interested in analysis and policy-relevant discussion of trade, investment, and development issues in the Asia-Pacific region.[2] While it was generally agreed at the first and subsequent conferences that a free trade area was not consistent with U.S. or regional foreign economic policy interests, there seemed considerable need and ample scope for institutional innovation and policy initiatives directed towards the broad objectives of extending and securing Asian-Pacific economic cooperation.

In its early form the OPTAD proposal was put forward by Australian and accepted by Japanese economists. Significantly, this and other concepts of regional economic association have been most widely discussed among the political, business and intellectual leadership in Japan and Australia.³ Thus far, no prominent elements in the bureaucracies of these two countries (nor in the United States) have been associated with the public advocacy of the OPTAD concept. The OPTAD proposal was recently endorsed in the Crawford-Okita Report to the Governments of Australia and Japan titled *Australia, Japan and Western Pacific Economic Relations*.⁴

The discussion of the OPTAD proposal in the context of the PAFTAD Conference series and more widely within Australia and Japan over the years reveals four broad goals. First, it was conceived to provide a more effective safety-valve, given the high existing levels of interdependence, for the discussion of trade and economic grievances among Pacific countries in a rational and cooperative atmosphere calculated not to damage profitable national trading interests. Second, it aimed to provide a stimulus to investment and aid flows for the developing countries of the Asian-Pacific region and a framework for improvement in the structure and quality of their aid, investment and trade relations with the developed countries in the Pacific. Third, it was to provide a forum for consultation and discussion about the longer term developments in and economic transformation of the region. A final but absolutely fundamental consideration was the role envisaged for OPTAD in providing a more secure framework of economic alliance among the countries of Asia and the Pacific, an alliance within which participants could feel free to develop closer economic integration in smaller groupings and through which participants could play a more constructive role in the expansion of relations with China, the Soviet Union, and the Indochina states following the Vietnam War.⁵

The establishment of an Organization for Pacific Trade and Development which served these aims could effectively weld together the three major strands, it was felt, in relationships among Asian-Pacific countries: the crucial economic links with Japan and the United States; the political, diplomatic, and economic involvements with the developing countries, both non-communist and communist, within the Western Pacific region; and the strategic interest in stable and constructive relationships among the major powers in East Asia and the Pacific.

In Japan, there have been various supporters of the concept of an Asian-Pacific regional economic association, at times from quite different perspectives. The dominant strand in support for the idea seeks, through a regional association, to consolidate Japan's relationship with the United States, while another element seeks to promote more strongly Japan's Asian leadership role. Some senior Cabinet Ministers in successive Japanese Governments have broadly endorsed the concept, most prominently former Prime Minister Miki. The prestigious Nomura Research Institute recently advocated a Pacific economic association in a forward and thought-provoking look at Japan's position in world affairs.[6] Former Nomura President Saeki argues that a Pacific association and the increased Japanese regional economic obligations that would go with it, comprise a key element in a comprehensive security strategy for Japan. Japan's contribution to comprehensive security should involve a much larger economic assistance and international development component compared with the military component, which will decline in relative importance for all countries.[7] In December 1978 the new Prime Minister Ohira offered general support for the idea of a "Pan Pacific association" on his accession to leadership, though what he envisages in detail is not yet clear. He has established a special task force to examine Japan's relations with the Pacific nations and the concept of a Pacific community under the chairmanship of Dr. Saburo Okita, one of the initial proponents of OPTAD.

In Australia, the OPTAD proposal has also enjoyed a measure of bipartisan support and was strongly endorsed by the Australian Senate's Joint Party standing Committee on Foreign Affairs and Defense.[8] The present Prime Minister (before his accession to leadership) has been attracted by the idea and the present Leader of the Opposition has put it forward as a major interest in Australian foreign policy.[9]

An important factor in Western Pacific support for the idea of a Pacific economic association, which commonly (though not always or inevitably) is envisaged as requiring U.S. participation, is a strong current of pro-American feeling. This derives both from Japanese and Australian conceptions of their own national interests in firm ties with the United States, and also follows from a sense of the importance of encouraging a revitalized U.S. presence and leadership in the Western Pacific economy.

There has been less American awareness of the U.S. interest in Asian-Pacific regional economic association but, as developments in the relationship with Japan have given prominence to the management of foreign economic policy towards the Pacific, awareness has been growing. In August 1977 the OPTAD idea was reviewed at the Ninth PAFTAD Conference at the Federal Reserve Bank of San Francisco.[10] It has also been endorsed in a forthcoming Brookings Institution study of economic interdependence in Asia and the Pacific,[11] and in a major lecture series underway at the School of Business, University of Washington.[12]

2. The U.S. Interest in Participation in an OPTAD

It is clear that proposals for some sort of regional economic association are a live issue in Japan, Australia, and elsewhere in the Western Pacific community. As the discussion above indicates, the United States has strong national interests in active participation in the discussions and any eventual formation of an OPTAD. A case can be made that the timing for American consideration of this issue now seems right. OPTAD could be a useful vehicle for the effective revitalization of U.S. economic leadership in the Asian-Pacific region. In asserting its commitment to the trade and development objectives of Asian-Pacific countries, the United States could insert its own conception of Pacific needs and interests alongside those of the Western Pacific countries. There is some evidence that Japan, and other Western Pacific countries, would welcome American active participation, and that the bilateral relationship with Japan would be strengthened rather than weakened. It seems possible that Japan and Australia, together with the ASEAN nations at the least, may decide in the future to move ahead on their own if the United States is not prepared to become involved. Such an action would further undermine U.S. influence and leadership in the region. The potential costs of not giving sufficient priority to the Asia-Pacific economic region may be rising sharply; at the least American national interests would appear to warrant a new evaluation and definition.

While participation in OPTAD may well be in the national interest of the United States, much depends on the basic purposes and principles of the organization. It would have to be compatible with and supportive of the U.S. global approach; it appears that the proponents of OPTAD, in contrast to those favoring a Pacific free trade area, do envisage it as supplementary to and supportive of a global framework. If perceived by the developing Asian-Pacific (or other) nations as a ganging up of Japan and the United States against their interests, OPTAD would be considered pernicious. It is unlikely that any such perception, much less actuality, of United States–Japan collusion would be in the long-run best interests of the United States regionally or globally.

The precise contours of an OPTAD are yet to be defined. Indeed, they may be expected to emerge firmly only from discussions among potential initial members. From an American perspective certain principles on membership and on OPTAD organizational structure seem worthy of preliminary consideration. In the next two sections these matters are considered.

3. Membership Options

Alternative geographic, political and economic definitions of the Asia-Pacific region are possible, depending upon the purposes of definition and criteria of selection. One way to classify the various components of the Asian-Pacific economy most broadly defined is in the following categories:

1. The fourteen major Pacific Basin market-oriented economies:
    (a) The five advanced countries: the United States, Japan, Australia, Canada, and New Zealand.

The OPTAD Proposal 159

    (b) The five ASEAN nations: Indonesia, Malaysia, the Philippines, Singapore, and Thailand.
    (c) The three Northeast Asian developing economies: South Korea, Taiwan, and Hong Kong.
    (d) Papua New Guinea and the small South West Pacific states as a group (the countries of the South Pacific Bureau for Economic Cooperation excluding Australia and New Zealand).
2. The South Asian nations: Bangladesh, Burma, India, Pakistan, Sri Lanka.
3. The Latin American Pacific nations: Mexico, the Central American states, Colombia, Ecuador, Peru, Chile, and in terms of economic interaction Brazil.
4. The Communist nations: China, Vietnam, Cambodia, Laos, North Korea, and the Soviet Union.

The preceding discussion suggests certain criteria for inclusion in the initial membership in OPTAD. One option for consideration is that the fundamental criterion be that members commit themselves to acceptance of an adherence to a system of fair, open, and multilateral competition within a free market framework for all international economic transactions, based upon accepted rules (to be worked out within OPTAD) for trade and commercial practices, aid terms and arrangements, and investment and capital flows including codes of conduct. In other words, the basic principle might be a commitment to an expansion of trade and investment opportunities, at least on a regional basis; this would be founded on the underlying perception that an institution such as OPTAD would be a useful vehicle for obtaining concrete, sensible mechanisms for encouraging economic interchange through OPTAD among countries with substantial overlapping economic relations.

Initial membership could be limited to nations the economies of which are arranged basically on market principles. Indeed, an initial joint effort could be directed at developing mechanisms to expand trade with the communist states in the region, including China. The organization would presumably include both economically advanced and developing market economies. At the same time, countries should have demonstrated a substantial community of regional interests through ongoing trade and other interactions. To make the negotiating process feasible, initial membership might well be limited to a relatively small number of countries.

These criteria suggest that initial membership could comprise as many of the fourteen Asia-Pacific market economies (category 1 above) as wish to join. However, the status of Taiwan as an independent national state is not recognized by most potential OPTAD members and Taiwan would require special treatment. The normalization of relations between the United States and China seems to imply an understanding from the side of the People's Republic of China of Taiwan's desire to preserve a different socio-economic structure and, from the side of the United States, acknowledgement of some form of political integration between the two countries. From the perspective of U.S. policy toward the Taiwan question a willingness to include Taiwan as a kind of observer would appear to provide some useful guarantees without necessarily compromising the priority of the relationship with China. Hong Kong, which is a British dependency, could also be admitted under observer status. The representation of the ministates within the South Pacific Bureau of Economic Cooperation, most likely by Papua New Guinea, is a question that also would have to be resolved.

Little benefit appears to derive from exclusive membership; others could be allowed, indeed encouraged, to participate in due course if they were willing to accept the basic principles, assumptions, and goals of OPTAD. Nor should the purpose of OPTAD necessarily be limited to the promotion of economic interchange only among Asian-Pacific economies. Accordingly, brief consideration of the relations of OPTAD to the other categories of nations is warranted.

The South Asian nations are not here included as candidates for initial membership. Their overwhelming population size, their special developmental problems as very low-income developing nations, and different external orientations, mean they have interests and concerns rather different from the other Asian-Pacific nations. These might prove difficult to accommodate in the initial establishment of OPTAD; to our knowledge there never has been any special interest in OPTAD manifested in South Asia nations. However, should membership in an OPTAD be mutually advantageous, they should not be excluded from joining eventually.

Latin American nations have not yet demonstrated a strong interest in the Asian-Pacific region, or in a regional organization such as OPTAD. Consciousness within the region is more Latin than specifically Atlantic or Pacific in nature. By the criterion of economic interaction rather than geography, Brazil, for example, is more a "Pacific" nation than some bordering on the Pacific. In due course various Latin American nations, both those bordering on the Pacific and others, may desire to join. Once established, OPTAD might well consider such membership requests favorably.

Clearly one of the major concerns of the United States, and indeed of all the market economies of the Asian-Pacific region, is how to establish an appropriate framework and suitable mechanisms for engaging in growing trade and other economic relations with the Communist nations of Asia. As socialist economies, they rely upon planning in domestic resource allocation and on state institutions for foreign trade. The recent

The OPTAD Proposal 161

changes in the development strategy and foreign economic orientation of China suggest the likelihood both of substantial new export opportunities and of new competition in import and third country markets for the United States and all other potential OPTAD members. In the longer run economic opportunities may develop in the Indochina subregion as well. Siberian natural resources constitute another potential for trade, though much depends on the future evolution of the U.S.S.R. political-economic strategy for the development of that part of the nation. Yet the Asian Communist states are currently involved in a complex set of competitive relationships, emanating in large part from the Sino-Soviet conflict. Obviously there is no monolithic communist bloc in Asia.

The major differences in economic system and approaches to international economic relations of the Communist nations, their internal and external political complexities, and indeed the entire realm of strategic concerns of the United States and others suggest it may not be wise to include the Communist nations in OPTAD membership. At the same time, OPTAD could be a particularly useful forum for consultations and even development of a concerted, coordinated approach to doing business with the Asian Communist states. Certainly no one should ignore the possibilities and opportunities that may arise, particularly in light of China's new policy stance.

4. Principles for an Organizational Structure for OPTAD

It may be premature to detail the precise organizational structure for OPTAD. However, these general principles of organization are suggested for consideration.

1. That OPTAD be a governmental organization, with its members the constituent governments.
2. That leadership of the United States and Japan, and the full involvement of Australia, South Korea, the non-communist Southeast Asian countries, and other Pacific Basin countries can best build the organizational structure.
3. That the administrative apparatus be small and not heavily bureaucratic.
4. That issues be handled by specific functional Task Forces with specified policy-oriented assignments, initiated through a high political-level consultative mechanism.
5. That the style of operations be consultative, informal, and communicative. An important function would be the exchange of information and ideas, as well as the initiation of negotiations on policy issues.

For purposes of discussion one might envisage:

1. A process of high-level political consultations initiated by a meet-

ing of the Heads of Government. Heads of Government or Ministerial level meetings should occur every one to two years and would provide one, but not the sole, vehicle for initiating Task Force assignments. Given the increasingly intensive consultation at Heads of Government level within the region, it is probable that these meetings could incorporate the participation of more and more Heads of Government.

2. A Steering Committee, meeting annually or more regularly, consisting of high-level representatives of member governments. In the case of the United States, the representative might be the Under Secretary of State for Economic Affairs, perhaps heading a delegation including an appropriate member of the Senate or House from the U.S. Congress.

3. A small permanent secretariat, staffed by senior professionals, perhaps on leave from the administrations of member governments or elsewhere. Apart from government representation, staffing would not be constrained at other levels by the interests of the various members. We suggest caution in imitating the broad functions and large staffing of the OECD.

4. The main staff work at OPTAD would be undertaken by functional Task Forces. Most would be established on an ad hoc basis to treat specific policy issues but some might become ongoing. The Task Force members and support staffs would be mobilized from the pools of professional expertise both within and outside member governments.

One extremely important problem is that of governance, in particular how to integrate the domestic political process and the legislative system into the formulation of policy for OPTAD. The problems and opportunities of economic interdependence at the regional as well as global level both influence and are influenced by domestic, political, and economic considerations in each member country, most certainly in the United States. The involvement of Congress is of particular importance in the U.S. context; its role in foreign economic policy is significant. The OPTAD structure should take account of and accommodate these national political processes. It thus seems to us important that Task Force members include from time to time professional expertise from the legislative staffs; and that similar methods be found to facilitate the flows of ideas and the debate on relevant policy issues. It would be useful for the secretariat at the least to maintain communications channels with legislative as well as executive branches. It might well be desirable that the annual meetings include representation from the Congress as well as the Executive Branch.

The creation of Task Forces would depend on the specific needs to be met through OPTAD. Possible among the policy areas upon which the Pacific Basin countries might focus their attention through OPTAD are:

1. *Task force on free and fair trade.* Its purpose would be to develop

The OPTAD Proposal

codes of business conduct, and mechanisms for their enforcement, which restrain corruption and other unfair practices, and which protect the capacity of sovereign governments to guarantee fair and free trade.

2. *Task force on trade restructuring.* Its purposes would be, in light of evolving industrial comparative advantage, competitiveness and specialization among the nations of the region, to develop mechanisms which safeguard and promote market access, and facilitate the adjustment process while reducing the social costs of change in those sectors losing competitive power. These could well involve concern with the issues of relocation of resource and energy-using industries, and would apply to market access and adjustment concerns in developing as well as advanced economy members.

3. *Task force on the financing of regional development.* Its main purpose would be to seek more effective access to and utilization of external resources for the developing countries of the region. This could include improved access to the Asian-dollar market, the Tokyo capital market, and other regional sources of capital as well as the established sources in the United States and Euro-dollar markets; and exploration of regional untieing of aid as a forerunner to global untieing.

4. *Task force on foreign direct investment.* Its purpose would be to enhance the opportunities for American and other advanced country investment in the region on a nonrestrictive and non-bilateral basis, while protecting the interests both of investors and host countries. One goal would be to develop an acceptable code for foreign investment.

5. *Task force on resource and energy security.* Its purpose would be to develop commitments to enhance energy security, to enhance energy research and development and to provide a forum for regional consultation on relevant resource and energy policy issues. In addition it, or one of the other task forces, could have a consultative role regarding possible stabilization programs for Pacific developing country commodity prices and output analogous to the European Common Market Stabex scheme.

6. *Task force on trade with the Communist States.* Its purpose would be to provide a forum for consultation and coordination in developing policies, rules, and mechanisms for trade with the various Asian Communist states.

NOTES

1. Peter Drysdale, "An Organization for Pacific Trade, Aid and Development: Regional Arrangements and the Resource Trade," in Lawrence B. Krause and Hugh T. Patrick, eds., *Minerals Resources in the Pacific* (San Francisco: Federal Reserve Bank of San Francisco, 1978), pp. 8-15.
2. A series of ten Pacific Trade and Development Conferences have been held

to date. The First Pacific Trade and Development Conference in Tokyo in January 1968 examined the Pacific Free Trade Area proposal and alternative trading arrangements. The Second Conference, in Honolulu a year later, considered explicitly the interests and needs of the developing nations of the Pacific; the Third conference was held in Sydney in August 1970 on issues of private direct investment in the Pacific region. A pattern Had emerged which has resulted in the continuing series and in the organization arrangements thereof. The Fourth Pacific Trade and Development Conference, on obstacles to trade in the Pacific area, was held in Ottawa in October 1971; the Fifth, on structural adjustments in Asian-Pacific trade, was held in Tokyo in January 1973; the Sixth, on technology transfer in Pacific economic development, was held in Mexico City in July 1974; the Seventh, on relations among the larger and smaller nations of the Pacific, was held in AUckland in August 1975; and the Eighth, on trade and employment, was held in Thailand in July 1976. The Ninth Pacific Trade and Development Conference, on the theme of the production, processing, financing, and trade of natural resources in the Pacific Basin, was held in San Francisco in August 1977. The Tenth, on ASEAN in the changing Pacific and world economy, was held in Canberra in March 1979. Conference papers and proceedings have been published, in sequence: Kiyoshi Kojima, ed., *Pacific Trade and Development*, Japan Economic Research Center, Tokyo, February 1968; Kiyoshi Kojima, ed., *Pacific Trade and Development II*, Japan Economic Research Center, Tokyo, April 1979; Peter Drysdale, ed., *Direct Foreign Investment in Asia and the Pacific*, Australian National University Press, Canberra, 1972; H. E. English and Keith Hay, eds., *Obstacles to Trade in the Pacific Area*, Carleton University, Ottawa, 1972; Kiyoshi Kojima, ed., *Structural Adjustments in Asian-Pacific Trade*, Japan Economic Research Center, Tokyo, August 1973; Kiyoshi Kojima and Miguel S. Wionczek, eds., *Technology Transfer in Pacific Economic Development*, Japan Economic Research Center, Tokyo, January 1975; L. V. Castle and Frank W. Holmes, eds., *Co-Operation and Development in the Asia-Pacific Region— Relations between Large and Small Countries*, Japan Economic Research Center, Tokyo, 1976; Narongchai Akrasanee et al., eds., *Trade and Employment in Asia and the Pacific*, University Press of Hawaii, Honolulu, 1977; and Krause and Patrick, *Mineral Resources*. A major joint research project undertaken by a group of Australian economists centered on the Australian National University and a group of Japanese economists working from the Japanese Economic Research Center under the direction of Sir John Crawford and Dr. Saburo Okita has published, and continues to publish, a considerable volume of work on Australia, Japan, and Western Pacific economic relations. See J. G. Crawford, Saburo Okita, et al., *Australia, Japan and Western Pacific Economic Relations: A Report to the Governments of Australia and Japan*, (Canberra: Australian Government Publisher, 1976) revised and published as Sir John Crawford and Saburo Okita, eds., *Raw Materials and Pacific Economic Integration* (London: Croom Helm, 1978).

3. Drysdale, "An Organization," p. 13.

The OPTAD Proposal

4. Crawford and Okita, *Australia, Japan.*
5. Drysdale, "An Organization," p. 14.
6. Kiichi Saeki, ed., *The Search for Japan's Comprehensive Policy Guideline in the Changing World—National Priorities for the 21st Century* (Kamakura: Nomura Research Institute, 1978).
7. Saeki, *The Search For Japan's Comprehensive Policy*, pp. 1-2.
8. Parliament of Australia, *Japan: Report from the Senate Standing Committee on Foreign Affairs and Defense*, (Canberra: Australian Government Publishing Service, 1971).
9. Address by the leader of the opposition, Mr. Bill Hayden, to the Australia-Japan Society, Sydney, August 1978.
10. Krause and Patrick, *Mineral Resources.*
11. Lawrence B. Krause and Sueo Sekiguchi, *Economic Interaction in the Pacific Basin* (Washington: Brookings Institution, forthcoming).
12. Lectures have included Krause, "The Pacific Economy" and Drysdale, "Australia's Economic Relations."

APPENDIX C
Summary of the Report on the Pacific Basin Cooperation Concept

Like the Patrick-Drysdale study, The Pacific Basin Cooperation Study Group Proposal is lengthy and detailed. A summary, prepared by the authors as part of the original document, is reprinted in full below.

I. The Pacific Basin Cooperation Concept
   1. Remarkable progress in communication and transport technologies has turned the vast Pacific Ocean into an inland sea and ordered conditions so that the Pacific countries can create a regional community. Indeed, the Pacific countries have already developed a variety of bilateral and multilateral cooperative relations, and there are moves afoot to put forth ideas of building a regional community among them.
   2. The Pacific Basin Cooperation Concept which we espouse, premised as it is upon these developments, is oriented toward the twenty-first century and intended to maximize the vast potential of this region, not simply for the benefit of the Pacific countries, but to enhance the well-being and prosperity of the human society as a whole.
   3. The Pacific region features two striking characteristics:
      i. Many of the countries in this region, whether industrialized countries or developing countries, are flush with vigor and dynamism and hold great potential.
      ii. The countries of this region are extremely diverse in stage of economic development and also in ethnic, cultural, religious, and other backgrounds.
   4. Upon this recognition, our concept has the following three features:
      i. It is by no means an exclusive and closed regionalism vis-à-vis states outside of the region. Seriously concerned

over the pale recently cast over the free and open international economic system grounded in the GATT [General Agreement on Tariffs and Trade] and IMF [International Monetary Fund] arrangements, we sincerely hope that the Pacific countries can capitalize upon their characteristic vigor and dynamism to become globalism's new supporters.

ii. Within the region as well, the concept aims at the creation of free and open interdependence. In the cultural sphere, exchanges are to be promoted with maximum respect for diversity; and in the economic sphere the free transaction of goods and capital is to be vigorously encouraged with utmost respect for the developing countries' situations and interests. With the industrialized countries taking the initiative in opening their markets further and extending their economic and technical cooperation and the developing countries making steady self-help efforts, this region has great potential for opening a new horizon for tackling the North-South problem.

iii. Our concept in no way conflicts with the cooperative bilateral and multilateral relations already existing in the region. Rather, the concept stands on the valuable achievement of these existing cooperations, having mutually complementary relations with them.

II. Tasks for Pacific Basin Cooperation

1. A variety of measures are possible and necessary in order to promote the Pacific Basin Cooperation Concept. Some are issues which should be taken up promptly, and others are long-term objectives; some should be dealt with jointly by the countries concerned and on others Japan should take the initiative for its own action.

2. Our report proposes a number of projects which should be advanced. In this summary, we will simply outline our conceptual framework and cite just a few projects by way of illustration.

3. Respect for diversity is central to our concept. Therefore, to nurture profound mutual understanding of this diversity among the peoples of the region is the first step in promoting this concept. This mutual understanding must be nurtured by various people at all levels.

For example, contacts among people should be encouraged through overseas study programs for the youth, "the University of the Seas" (programs for study on board), and homestay programs, and also mutual understanding among people should be enhanced through "Pacific Basin Exhibitions" and other festivals held to introduce each other's cultural traditions, artistic products, and ways of life among the countries of the region.

Tourism's potential for enhancing mutual understanding should also be reconsidered and the arrangement of "working holidays" and the like promoted.

4. Japanese universities must substantially be internationalized in order to promote educational and academic exchange in the region. In this connection, it is, for example, extremely important that discrimination against foreign teaching staff at national universities be eliminated, that internationally open graduate schools be established, that regional studies be promoted.

5. The arrangements for the industrialized countries' extending cooperation for human resources development and technical cooperation must be strengthened in order to counter the lack of trained personnel which is a major impediment to the developing countries' development.

One way in which Japan could contribute further in this area would be to establish a "Technical Cooperation Center" and thus to sharply improve the present system under which specialists are dispatched on an ad hoc basis as part of their domestic duties.

6. In order to promote expanded and coordinated trade in the Pacific region and to seek positive adjustment of industrial structures in the region, the countries concerned should draw up a "Pacific Declaration on Trade and International Investment" to make clear their guiding principles. In this declaration, the industrialized countries should pledge to open their markets further as by liberalizing trade or reducing the tariff and nontariff barriers to trade. The developing countries on the other hand are expected to pledge, among others, to improve the climate for international investment.

At the same time, we propose the establishment of a "Pacific Industrial Policy Consultative Forum" to deliberate actual implementation of these guiding principles.

Japan especially, recognizing that contributing to the development of this entire region is very much to Japan's own medium- and long-term interest, should work to expand imports of tropical agricultural commodities and other products

of interest to the exporting countries and to promote technology transfer to the newly industrializing countries.
7. There are many areas in which the countries concerned should cooperate for the development of the Pacific Basin's abundant resources.

   For example, one very challenging task would be to implement a "Joint Pacific Oceanic Scientific Survey" as a first step to utilizing the nearly infinite resources contained within this vast ocean.

   Other attractive project areas include the joint use of satellites for resource exploration and such joint energy development as for nuclear power, liquefied or gasified coal, solar energy, and biomass.

   Agricultural cooperation such as for joint projects to enhance rice production, forestry cooperation such as to develop and utilize unused species of trees, and fishery cooperation such as to promote more effective use of marine resources are other important areas.
8. The smooth flow of capital in the region is an indispensable prerequisite to carrying out a variety of projects.

   The development of international finance and capital markets in the region is thus important, and Japan must take the initiative in promoting the opening or liberalization of its financial and capital markets as by easing direct and indirect restrictions, reducing negotiated transactions, or liberalizing interest rates.

   While the U.S. dollar will continue to be an important international currency, measures should also be taken in expectation of a greater international role for the yen.

   Moreover, it is also important that the investment climate be improved as through the expansion of financial institutions in the region and the conclusion of investment protection agreements.
9. The remarkable technical innovations made recently in the transport and communication sectors have yet to be fully utilized in the Pacific region.

   On air transportation, it is imperative that regional and island-feeder routes as well as North-South and East-West trunk routes be fully organized and that fare schedules be adjusted to suit the region's diverse passenger and cargo transport needs.

   On communication, we should work for the revision of fare schedules and the enhancement of the Pacific communication network, expecting such new technological developments as the glass fiber communications cable. Consideration should also be given to the dream of launching a direct-broadcast relay satellite to serve the entire region.

Moreover, we must also actively promote the internationalization of mass media systems, and immigration and foreign residents control systems.

III. Toward Realizing Pacific Basin Cooperation
1. This concept of forming a community in a region so much replete with potential and diversity is without historical precedent, a fact which bears witness both to the task's great attraction and to its difficulty. Pacific Basin cooperation should not be promoted hastily, but carefully and steadily through the gradual congealing of broad international consensus.
2. It is expected that the seminar to be held this September at Australian National University will become an important one of a continuing series of international conferences. For the time being, we hope that a nongovernmental committee of fifteen to twenty experts from the countries concerned will be established as a steering body to manage such conferences.

After a number of such conferences have been held, this committee might take on the characteristics of a permanent organization for Pacific Basin cooperation, and the committee might be able to express joint opinions or make recommendations to the governments concerned on matters where a consensus is reached among the conference participants.
3. Apart from this committee, it is also extremely useful for realizing Pacific Basin cooperation that working groups of specialists be formed at the governmental or private-sector levels to promote projects in specific areas, as have already been seen in the region.
4. The next step might be to examine the possibility of establishing an international organization for Pacific Basin cooperation among the governments of the countries concerned.

SELECTED READINGS

The following list of suggested readings has been compiled with the general reader in mind. It cites only representative books and articles prepared over approximately the past fifteen years and endeavors to avoid the more technical materials produced by research centers and such ongoing research projects as the Pacific Trade and Development Conferences, the Japanese-Australian Project, and the Australia-Japan Economic Relations Research Project. Readers seeking historical references should consult such bibliographies as Michael Haas (comp.), *International Organization: An Interdisciplinary Bibliography* (Stanford, 1973), while those interested in technical studies should consult the bibliography in John Grenfell Crawford and Saburo Okita (eds.), *Raw Materials and Pacific Economic Integration* (London, 1978).

Arndt, H. W., and Boxer, A. H., eds. *The Australian Economy.* Melbourne, 1972.
Asian Development Bank. *South East Asia's Economy in the 1970s.* London, 1971.
Auer, James E. "Toward a Pacific Maritime Union: Resolving the Japan-U.S. Security Treaty Dilemma." *Pacific Community* 5 (October 1973):53–67.
Awanohara, Susumu. "Clearing Hurdles in the Pacific." *Far Eastern Economic Review,* February 1, 1980.
Bull, Headly, ed. *Asia and the Western Pacific: Towards A New International Order.* Sydney, 1975.
Center for Strategic and International Studies. *CSIS Conference on Asia-Pacific in the 1980s: Toward Greater Symmetry in Economic Interdependence.* Jakarta, 1980.
———. *Japanese-Indonesia Relations in the Seventies.* Jakarta, 1974.
Cleveland, Harlan. "The Atlantic Analogy." *Pacific Community* 3 (October 1971):42–52.

Cooper, Richard N., ed. *A Re-Ordered World: Emerging International Economic Problems.* Washington, 1973.
Corbet, Hugh, and Jackson, Robert, eds. *In Search of a New World Economic Order.* London, 1974.
Crawford, Sir John Grenfell. *Australian Trade Policy 1942-1966: A Documentary History.* Canberra, 1968.
Crawford, Sir John Grenfell, and Okita, Saburo. *Australia, Japan and Western Pacific Economic Relations.* Canberra, 1976.
_____, eds. *Raw Materials and Pacific Economic Integration.* London, 1978.
Davies, Derek. "Exploiting the Pacific Tide." *Far Eastern Economic Review*, December 21, 1979.
Dibb, Paul. "The Strategic Interrelations of the U.S., the U.S.S.R. and China in the East Asia-Pacific Area." *Australian Outlook* 32 (August 1978):169-181.
Edwards, John. "Moulding a New Community." *Far Eastern Economic Review*, August 22, 1980.
Ester, Helen. "Slow Start in the Pacific." *Far Eastern Economic Review*, September 26, 1980.
Far Eastern Economic Review. *Asia Yearbook.* Hongkong, 1973-.
_____. *Far Eastern Economic Review Yearbook.* Hongkong, 1960-1972.
Grant, Margaret, ed. *South Asia Pacific Crisis.* New York, 1964.
Hernadi, Andras. "Pacific Region as a Growth Sub-Center and Japan's Role." *Asia Pacific Community*, no. 5 (Summer 1979):109-128.
Hewett, Robert H., ed. *Future Economic and Security Cooperation in the Pacific Region: A Private Conference of the Pacific Forum.* Honolulu, 1979.
Johnson, U. Alexis. "The Pacific Basin." *Pacific Community* 1 (October 1969):11-19.
Jorgensen-Dahl, Arnfin. "Extra-Regional Influences on Regional Cooperation in S.E. Asia." *Pacific Community* 8 (April 1977):412-429.
Kahn, Herman. *The Emerging Japanese Superstate: Challenge and Response.* Englewood Cliffs, N.J., 1971.
Kanahele, George S., and Haas, Michael. "Prospects for a Pacific Community." *Pacific Community* 6 (October 1974):83-93.
Knight, John. "Australia and Proposals for Regional Consultation and Co-operation in the Asia and Pacific Era." *Australian Outlook* 28 (December 1974):259-273.
Kojima, Kiyoshi. *Economic Cooperation in a Pacific Community.* Japan Institute of International Affairs: Project '80s: Foreign Policy Guidelines of Japan. Tokyo, 1980.
_____. *Japan and a New World Economic Order.* London, 1977.
_____, ed. *Economic Cooperation in the Western Pacific.* Tokyo, 1973.

———. "A Pacific Free Trade Area Proposed." *Pacific Community* 3 (April 1972):585-596.
———. *Japan and a Pacific Free Trade Area*. London, 1971.
———, ed. *Second Pacific Trade and Development Conference Papers and Proceedings*. Tokyo, 1969.
———, ed. *First Pacific Trade and Development Conference Papers and Proceedings*. Tokyo, 1968.
Kojima, Kiyoshi, and Kurimoto, Hiroshi. "A Pacific Economic Community and Asian Developing Countries." *Hitotsubashi Journal of Economics* 7 (June 1966):17-37.
Kolde, Endel-Jakob. *The Pacific Quest: The Concept and Scope of an Oceanic Community*. Pacific Rim Research Series, no. 1. Lexington, Mass., 1976.
Krause, Lawrence B., and Sekiguchi, Sueo, eds. *Economic Interaction in the Pacific Basin*. Washington, 1980.
Kux, Ernst. "Is Russia a Pacific Power?" *Pacific Community* 1 (April 1970):498-510.
Macrae, Norman. "Pacific Century, 1975-2075?" *The (London) Economist*, January 4, 1975.
Miki, Takeo. *An Asian-Pacific Sphere*. Tokyo, 1967.
Millar, T. B. "Japan and Australia: Partners in the Pacific." *Pacific Community* 8 (October 1976):28-42.
Nixon, Richard M. "Asia After Vietnam." *Foreign Affairs* 46 (October 1967):111-125.
Okita, Saburo. "Japan, China and the United States: Economic Relations and Prospects." *Foreign Affairs* 57 (Summer 1979):1090-1110.
———. "Natural Resource Dependency and Japanese Foreign Policy." *Foreign Affairs* 52 (July 1974):714-724.
Overholt, William H. "The Rise of the Pacific Basin." *Pacific Community* 5 (July 1974): 516-533.
Pacific Basin Cooperation Study Group. *Report on the Pacific Basin Cooperation Concept*. Report to the Prime Minister, May 19, 1980. Tokyo: Office of the Prime Minister, 1980.
Pelaez, Emmanuel. "One Asia: The Quest for Unity." *Pacific Community* 2 (April 1971):577-588.
Ping, Lee Poh. "Reflections on the Pacific Community Concept." *Asic Pacific Community*, no. 8 (Spring 1980), pp. 35-43.
Ravenal, Earl C. "The New Strategic Balance in Asia." *Asia Pacifi Community*, no. 2 (Fall 1978), pp. 92-116.
Saeki, Kiichi, ed. *The Search for Japan's Comprehensive Policy Guide line in the Changing World: National Priorities for the 21st Cer tury*. Kamakura, 1978.
Sato, Eisaku. "Pacific Asia." *Pacific Community* 1 (October 1969):1-3

Soloman, Robert, and Gault, Anne. *The Interdependence of Nations: An Agenda for Research*. A Report to the National Science Foundation by the Brookings Institution. Washington, 1977.

Stockwin, Arthur, ed. *Japan and Australia in the Seventies*. Sydney, 1972.

Tokuyama, Jiro. "The Advantages of a Pacific Economic Basin." *Far Eastern Economic Review*, March 23, 1979.

Truitt, J. Frederick. "Canada and the Pacific Rim: Least Pacific or Most Pacific." *Pacific Community* 7 (January 1977):259–276.

United Nations, Economic and Social Commission for Asia and the Pacific. *Economic and Social Survey of Asia and the Pacific*. Bangkok, 1974–.

_____. *Statistical Yearbook for Asia and the Pacific*. Bangkok, 1973–.

U.S., Congress, House, Subcommittee on Asian and Pacific Affairs, *Hearings: The Pacific Community Idea*, 96th Cong., 1st sess., 1979.

U.S., Congress, Senate, Committee on Foreign Relations, *An Asian-Pacific Regional Economic Organization: An Exploratory Concept*, 96th Cong., 1st sess., 1979.

Wilson, Dick. "Economic Co-operation Within ASEAN." *Pacific Community* 5 (October 1973):80–96.